GARDEN CLUB QUILTS

Leisure Arts is delighted to present this collection of garden-inspired quilting projects from the Country Threads Quilt Shop. Experienced quilters will enjoy piecing and appliqueing the rows and patches of sweet blossoms, fresh vegetables, twinkling stars, handy baskets, happy birds, and lots of golden sunshine! Refer to the General Instructions on page 112 before beginning. The large Garden Club Quilt and its twelve very special companion pieces were all "grown" from brushed cotton fabrics in warm, earthy colors. You can plant a touch of softness on your table with place mats and a tea cozy or reap wall hangings by the bushel. And, whether you keep all of your harvest or share the bounty with a neighbor, you'll have the reassurance that this season's crop will last for many years to come. Happy stitching!

LEISURE ARTS, INC
Little Rock, Arkansas

EDITORIAL STAFF

Vice President and Editor-in-Chief:
 Sandra Graham Case
Executive Director of Publications:
 Cheryl Nodine Gunnells
Director of Designer Relations: Debra Nettles
Publications Director: Kristine Anderson Mertes
Editorial Director: Susan Frantz Wiles
Photography Director: Lori Ringwood Dimond
Art Operations Director: Jeff Curtis

PRODUCTION
Managing Editor: Cheryl R. Johnson
Senior Technical Writer: Sherry Solida Ford
Technical Writer: Jean W. Lewis

EDITORIAL
Managing Editor: Suzie Puckett
Associate Editor: Susan McManus Johnson

ART
Senior Art Director: Rhonda Hodge Shelby
Senior Production Artist: Lora Puls
Production Artist: Dana Vaughn
Color Technician: Mark Hawkins
Photography Stylists: Sondra Daniel and Cassie Newsom
Staff Photographer: Russell Ganser
Publishing Systems Administrator: Becky Riddle
Publishing Systems Assistants: Myra S. Means and
 Chris Wertenberger

BUSINESS STAFF

Publisher: Rick Barton
Vice President, Finance: Tom Siebenmorgen
Director of Corporate Planning and Development:
 Laticia Mull Cornett
Vice President, Retail Marketing: Bob Humphrey
Vice President, Sales: Ray Shelgosh

Vice President, National Accounts: Pam Stebbins
Director of Sales and Services: Margaret Sweetin
Vice President, Operations: Jim Dittrich
Comptroller, Operations: Rob Thieme
Retail Customer Service Manager: Wanda Price
Print Production Manager: Fred F. Pruss

Softcover ISBN 1-57486-251-0

10 9 8 7 6 5 4 3 2 1

1. Summer Glory

Basket Block

Add ¼" seam allowances to ALL templates.

Cutting guide – make 1.

Piece	Color	Cut;
No. 1	Green	1 square 16½" x 16½"
A	Cream	1 from template A
B	Cream	1 from template B
C	Red	1 from template C
D	Black	1 from template D
E	Orange	1 from template E
F	Gold	1 from template F
G	Yellow	1 from template G
H	Brown	1 from template H
I	Green	1 from template I
J	Green	1 from template J
K	Green	1 from template K
L	Gold	1 from template L
M	Blue	1 from template M
N	Black	1 from template N

Referring to the diagram, appliqué pieces A–N onto the green background square (No. 1).

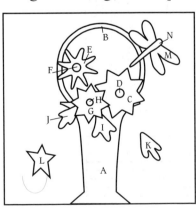

Basket Block
Make 1
Finished Size:
16" x 16"

Stars and Flowers Block

Add ¼" seam allowances to ALL templates.

5" SAWTOOTH STARS
Cutting guide for *each* block – make 2.

Piece	Color	Cut:
No. 1	Dark	1 square 3" x 3"
No. 2	Dark	8 squares 1¾" x 1¾"
No. 3	Light	4 rectangles 1¾" x 3"
No. 4	Light	4 squares 1¾" x 1¾"
A	Gold	1 from template A

For each block, use squares (No. 2) and rectangles (No. 3) to make 4 Flying Geese. Assemble the Flying Geese and the remaining squares to make the Sawtooth Square Block. Appliqué piece A onto the center of one block.

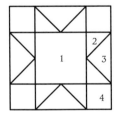

5" Sawtooth Star Block
Make 2
Finished Size: 5" x 5"

3" SAWTOOTH STARS
Cutting guide for *each* block – make 2.

Piece	Color	Cut:
No. 1	Dark	1 square 2" x 2"
No. 2	Dark	8 squares 1¼" x 1¼"
No. 3	Light	4 rectangles 1¼" x 2"
No. 4	Light	4 squares 1¼" x 1¼"

For each block, use squares (No. 2) and rectangles (No. 3) to make 4 Flying Geese. Assemble the Flying Geese and the remaining squares to make the Sawtooth Square Block.

3" Sawtooth Star Block
Make 2
Finished Size: 3" x 3"

FLOWER BLOCKS
Cutting guide for 2 blocks.

Piece	Color	Cut:
No. 1	Cream	1 square 3½" x 3½"
No. 2	Blue	1 square 3½" x 3½"
B	Red	1 from template B
B	Yellow	1 from template B

Appliqué 1 flower onto each square (No. 1) to make Flower Blocks.

SPACERS

Piece	Color	Cut:
No. 3	Yellow	1 rectangle 3½" x 5½"
No. 4	Blue	1 rectangle 3½" x 5½"
No. 5	Blue	1 rectangle 2½" x 6½"

Referring to the diagram, sew the Sawtooth Star Blocks, Flower Blocks, and Spacers together to make the Stars and Flowers Block.

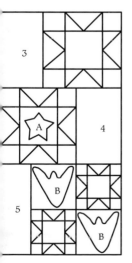

Stars and Flowers Block
Make 1
Finished Size: 8" x 16"

Flag Block

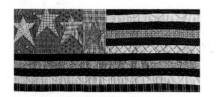

Add ¼" seam allowances to ALL templates.

Using templates 1-9 and referring to the photo for fabric colors, use 4 different background fabrics and 4 different star fabrics to make 4 Star Blocks.

Cut spacers for stars as follows:
Star 1 - 2 rectangles 1½" x 3½"
Star 2 - 1 rectangle 2½" x 3½"
Star 3 - 2 rectangles 1½" x 3½"
Star 4 - 1 rectangle 2½" x 3½"

From a variety of cream fabrics:
Cut 3 stripes 1½" x 12½"
Cut 2 stripes 1½" x 24½"

From a variety of red fabrics:
Cut 3 stripes 1½" x 12½"
Cut 3 stripes 1½" x 24½"

Referring to the diagram, sew the Star Blocks, spacers, and stripes together to make the Flag Block.

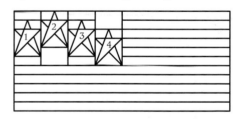

Flag Block
Make 1
Finished Size:
11" x 24"

Sew the Basket, Stars and Flowers, and Flag Blocks together to complete Section 1.

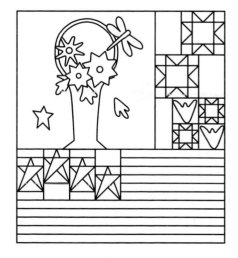

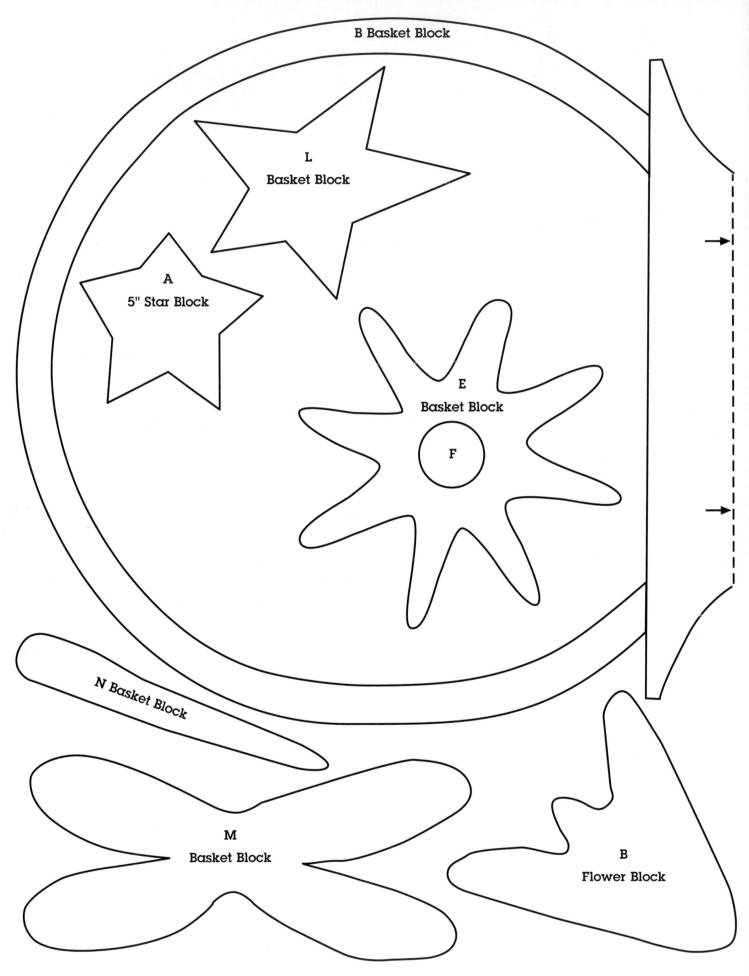

B Basket Block

L
Basket Block

A
5" Star Block

E
Basket Block

F

N Basket Block

M
Basket Block

B

Flower Block

8

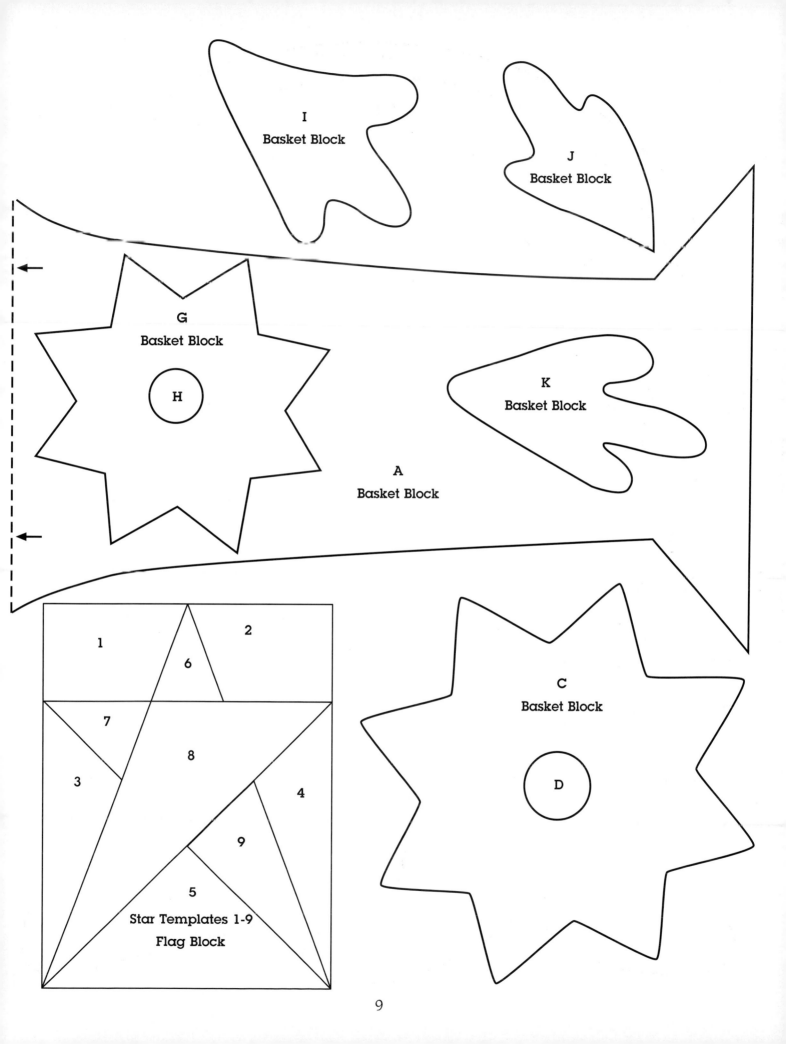

I
Basket Block

J
Basket Block

G
Basket Block

H

K
Basket Block

A
Basket Block

1
2
6
7
8
3
4
9
5

Star Templates 1-9
Flag Block

C
Basket Block

D

9

2. Bird Housing

Birdhouse Block

Add $1/4$" seam allowances to ALL templates.

Cutting guide – make 1.

Piece	Color	Cut:
No. 1	Cream	2 rectangles $3^1/4$" x $6^1/2$"
No. 2	Cream	1 square $6^1/2$" x $6^1/2$"
No. 3	Cream	1 rectangle $4^1/2$" x $8^1/2$"
No. 4	Cream	1 rectangle 4" x $11^1/2$"
No. 5	Brown	1 rectangle 1" x $6^1/2$"
No. 6	Brown	1 rectangle $3^1/2$" x $6^1/2$"
No. 7	Burgundy	1 rectangle $4^1/2$" x $6^1/2$"
No. 8	Green	1 rectangle 1" x $11^1/2$"
A	Green	1 from template A
B	Green	1 from template B
C	Rust	1 from template C
D	Green	1 from template D
E	Blue	1 from template E
F	Black	1 from template F
G	Gold	1 from template G

Referring to the diagram, appliqué tree A onto rectangle (No. 3); appliqué tree B and chimney C onto rectangle (No. 2). Sew rectangles (Nos. 4 and 8) together; appliqué the bird (E, F, and G). Sew rectangles (Nos. 1 and 5) together; add rectangles (Nos. 6 and 7). Appliqué the birdhouse hole (D). Sew the pieced and appliquéd units together to make the Birdhouse Block.

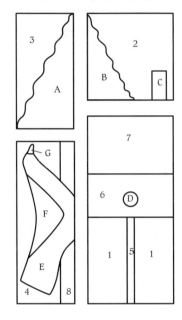

Birdhouse Block
Make 1
Finished Size: 10" x 19"

Spacer

Cut $1^1/2$" x $2^1/2$" rectangles from 10 different fabrics. Sew long edges together to make spacer.

Spacer
Make 1
Finished Size: 2" x 10"

Dutch Tulip Block

Add ¼" seam allowances to ALL templates.

Cutting guide – make 1.

Piece	Color	Cut:
No. 1	Green	1 square 10½" x 10½"
A	Light	1 from template A
B	Blue	2 from template B
C	Teal	4 from template C
D	Gold	4 from template D
E	Red	4 from template E

Referring to the diagram, appliqué pieces (A-E) onto the background square (No. 1) to make the Dutch Tulip Block.

Dutch Tulip Block
Make 1
Finished Size: 10" x 10"

Referring to the diagram, sew the Birdhouse Block, Spacer, and Dutch Tulip Block together to complete Section 2.

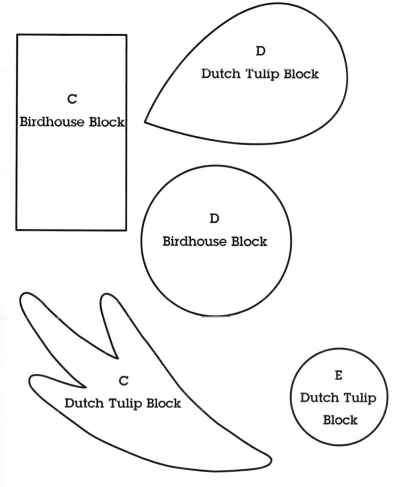

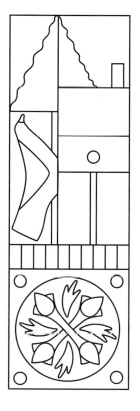

11

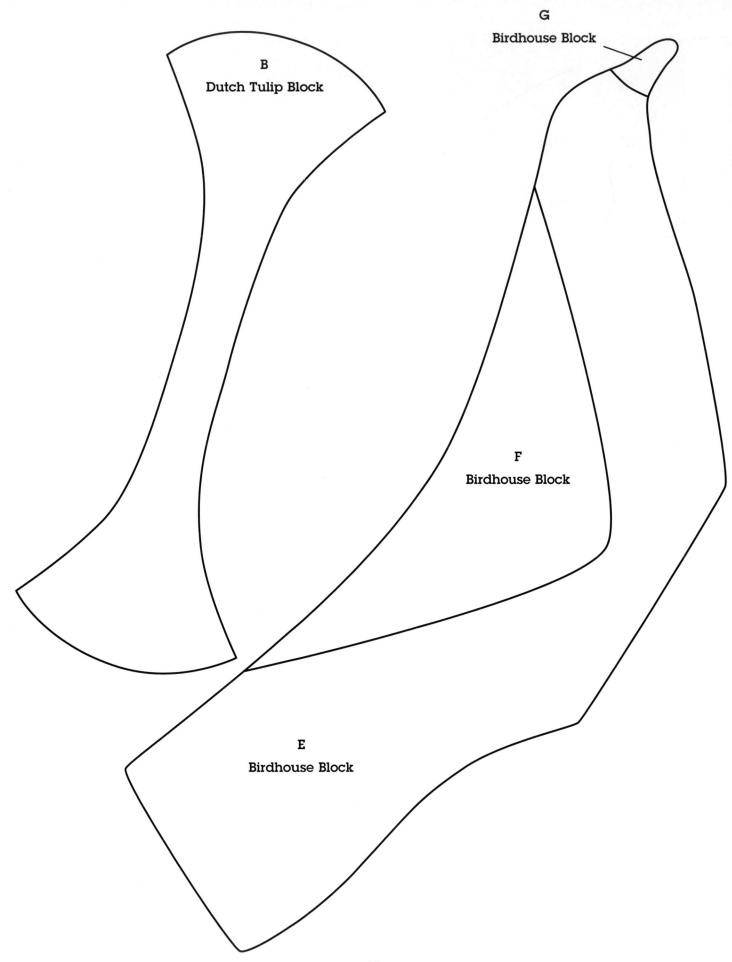

B
Dutch Tulip Block

G
Birdhouse Block

F
Birdhouse Block

E
Birdhouse Block

12

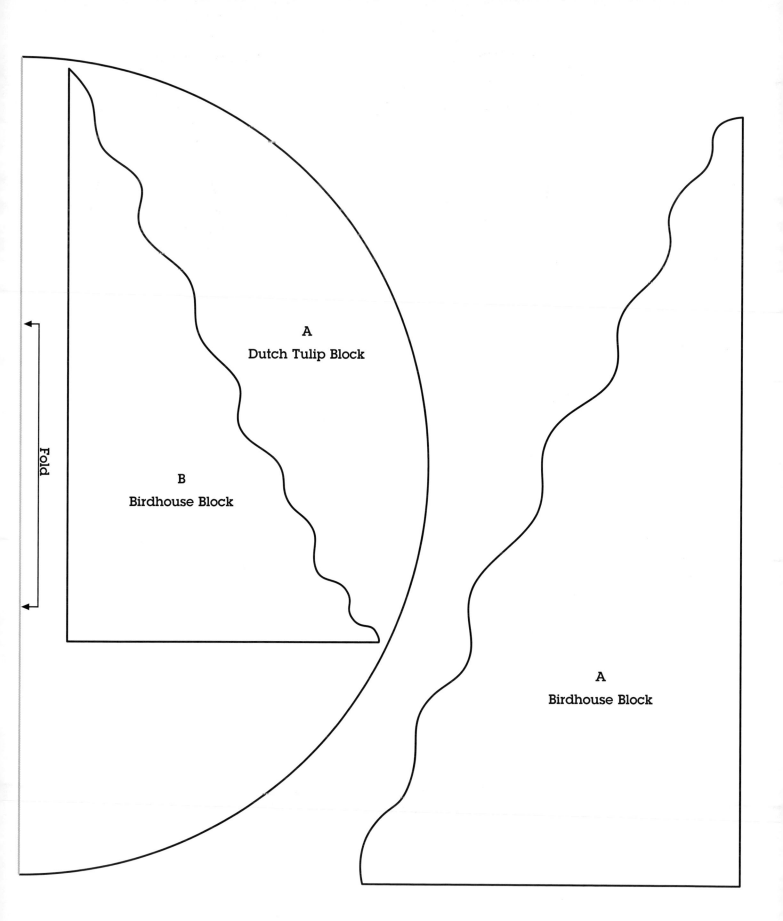

A
Dutch Tulip Block

B
Birdhouse Block

Fold

A
Birdhouse Block

13

3. Watering Can

Watering Can Block

Add ¹/₄" seam allowances to ALL templates.

Cutting guide – make 1.

Piece	Color	Cut:
No. 1	Tan	1 rectangle $3^1/_2$" x $11^1/_2$"
No. 2	Tan	1 rectangle 3" x $11^1/_2$"
No. 3	Light	1 rectangle $4^1/_2$" x 5"
No. 4	Blue	2 rectangles $1^1/_4$" x 5"
No. 5	Navy	1 rectangle 5" x 6"
A	Navy	1 from template A
B	Navy	1 from template B
C	Navy	1 from template C
D	Navy	1 from template D
E	Orange	1 from template E
F	Red	1 from template F

Referring to the diagram, appliqué pieces A and D onto rectangle (No. 1); piece B onto rectangle (No. 3), piece C onto rectangle (No. 2), and pieces E and F onto rectangle (No. 5). Sew rectangles together to make the Watering Can Block.

Dog Block

Add ¹/₄" seam allowances to ALL templates.

Cutting guide – make 1.

Piece	Color	Cut:
No. 1	Gold	1 rectangle $1^3/_4$" x $5^1/_2$"
No. 2	Gold	1 rectangle $2^1/_2$" x $14^1/_2$"
No. 3	Gold	1 rectangle $1^1/_2$" x 5"
No. 4	Gold	1 rectangle 2" x $2^1/_4$"
No. 5	Gold	1 square 1" x 1"
No. 6	Brown	1 rectangle $5^1/_2$" x $8^1/_4$"
No. 7	Brown	1 rectangle $1^3/_4$" x $2^3/_4$"
No. 8	Brown	1 rectangle $1^1/_4$" x $2^1/_4$"
No. 9	Brown	1 rectangle $2^1/_4$" x $3^1/_4$"
No. 10	Black	1 rectangle $2^3/_4$" x $4^1/_4$"
No. 11	Black	1 square 1" x 1"
A	Black	1 from template A
B	Black	1 from template B

Appliqué piece A to rectangle (No. 6). Referring to the diagram, sew rectangles and squares (Nos. 1-11) together and appliqué piece B in place to make the Dog Block.

Do not sew the two blocks together at this time.

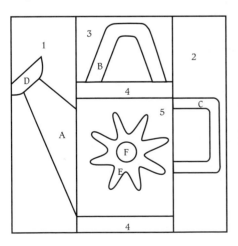

Watering Can Block
Make 1
Finished Size:
10" x 11"

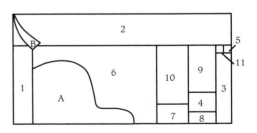

Dog Block
Make 1
Finished Size: 7" x 14"

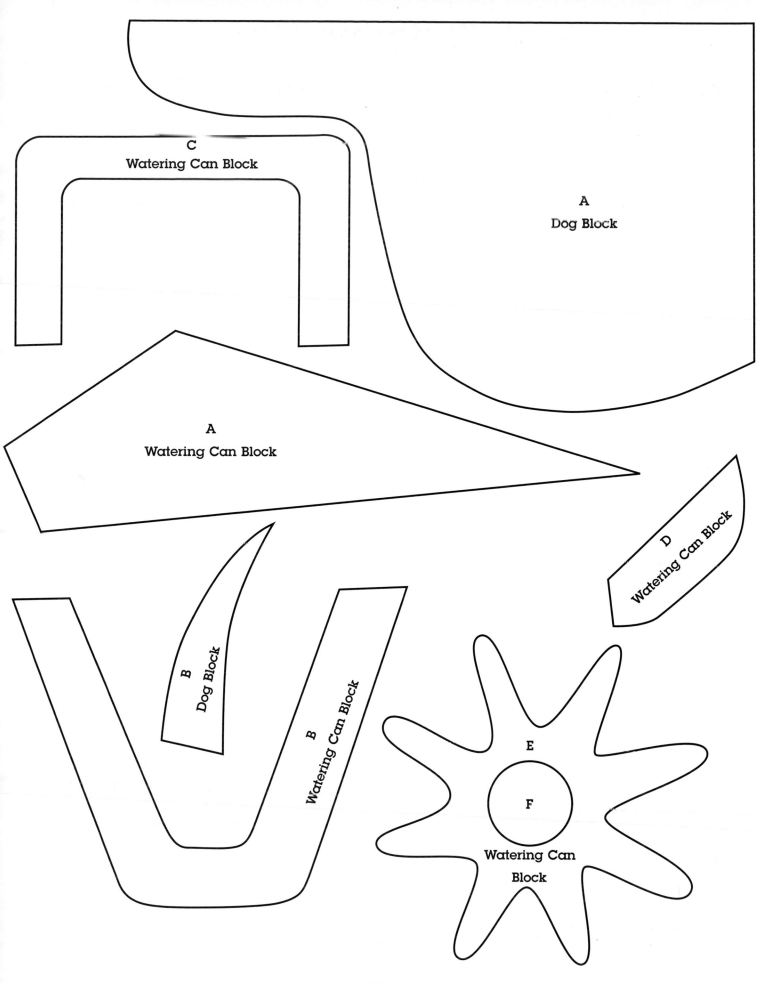

C
Watering Can Block

A
Dog Block

A
Watering Can Block

D
Watering Can Block

B
Dog Block

B
Watering Can Block

E

F

Watering Can
Block

4. Gimme Flowers

Potted Tree Block

Add ¼" seam allowances to ALL templates.

Cutting guide – make 1.

Piece	Color	Cut:
No. 1	Tan	1 rectangle 6½" x 16½"
A	Green	1 from template A
B	Black	1 from template B
C	Orange	1 from template C
D	Orange	1 from template D

Referring to the diagram, appliqué pieces A-D onto the tan background rectangle (No. 1) to make the Potted Tree Block.

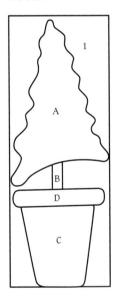

Potted Tree Block
Make 1
Finished Size: 6" x 16"

Trug Block

Add ¼" seam allowances to ALL templates.

Cutting guide – make 1.

Piece	Color	Cut:
No. 1	Tan	1 rectangle 7½" x 12½"
A	Cream	1 from template A
B	Cream	1 and 1(R) from template B
C	Orange	1 from template C
D	Orange	1 from template D
E	Blue	1 from template E

Referring to the diagram, appliqué pieces A-E onto the tan background rectangle (No. 1). Referring to the photo for placement, use brown embroidery floss and a running stitch to work 2 lines across the trug to indicate slates.

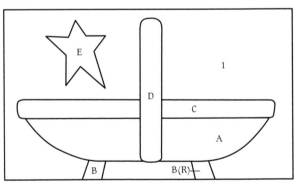

Trug Block
Make 1
Finished Size: 7" x 12"

Spacer (not shown)

From assorted fabrics, cut 3 squares 2½" x 2½"; sew together into a row to make the Spacer. Sew the Spacer to the top of the Potted Tree Block.

Tulip Blocks

Add ¼" seam allowances to ALL templates.

Cutting guide for *each* block – make 5.

Piece	Color	Cut:
No. 1	Cream	1 rectangle 1½" x 2½"
No. 2	Cream	1 rectangle 1" x 1½"
No. 3	Cream	1 rectangle 1½" x 2"
No. 4	Cream	1 square 1½" x 1½"
No. 5	Red	2 squares 1½" x 1½"
No. 6	Red	1 rectangle 1" x 2½"
No. 7	Green	2 squares 1½" x 1½"
No. 8	Tan	4 rectangles 1" x 3½"
A	Green	5 from template A

For each block, use rectangles (No. 1) and squares (No. 5) to make one Flying Geese block; sew rectangle (No. 6) to the bottom of the block. Stitch diagonally, trim, and flip to sew one square (No. 7) each to rectangle (No. 3) and square (No. 4). Referring to the diagram, assemble the pieced sections. Appliqué the stem (A) in place to complete one Tulip Block. Make a total of 5 Tulip Blocks. Sew blocks and rectangles (No. 8) together to make the Tulip Row.

Tulip Block
Make 5
Finished Size: 2" x 3"

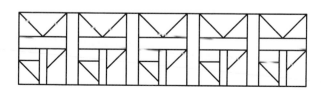

Tulip Row
Make 1
Finished Size: 3" x 12"

Star Block

Add ¼" seam allowances to ALL templates.

Cutting guide – make 1.

Piece	Color	Cut:
1-5	Tan	1 each from templates 1-5
6-9	Red	1 each from templates 6-9

Referring to the diagram, sew pieces 1-9 together to make the Star Block.

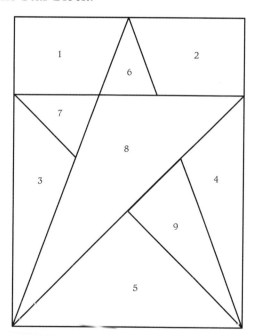

Star Block
Make 1
Finished Size: 6" x 8"

1-Hole Birdhouse Block

Add ¼" seam allowances to ALL templates.

Cutting guide – make 1.

Piece	Color	Cut:
No. 1	Brown	1 rectangle 3¼" x 4½"
No. 2	Blue	1 rectangle 2½" x 4½"
A	Black	1 from template A

Appliqué piece A to rectangle (No. 2). Referring to the diagram, sew rectangles (Nos. 1 and 2) together to make the 1-Hole Birdhouse Block.

1-Hole Birdhouse Block
Make 1
Finished Size: 4" x 4¾"

2-Hole Birdhouse Block

Add ¼" seam allowances to ALL templates.

Cutting guide – make 1.

Piece	Color	Cut:
No. 1	Green	1 rectangle 5¾" x 4½"
No. 2	Cream	2 squares 2½" x 2½"
B	Gold	2 from template B

Appliqué pieces (B) to rectangle (No. 1). Stitch diagonally, trim, and flip to sew squares (No. 2) to rectangle (No. 1) to make the 2-Hole Birdhouse Block.

2-Hole Birdhouse Block
Make 1
Finished Size: 4" x 4¾"

Trowel Block

Piece	Color	Cut:
No. 1	Tan	1 rectangle 3¾" x 8½"
A	Brown	1 from template A
B	Green	1 from template B

Referring to the diagram, appliqué pieces A and B onto rectangle (No. 1) to make the Trowel Block.

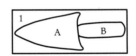

Trowel Block
Make 1
Finished Size: 3¼" x 8"

Do not sew the section pieces together at this time.

E
Trug Block

B
Trug Block

D
Trug Block

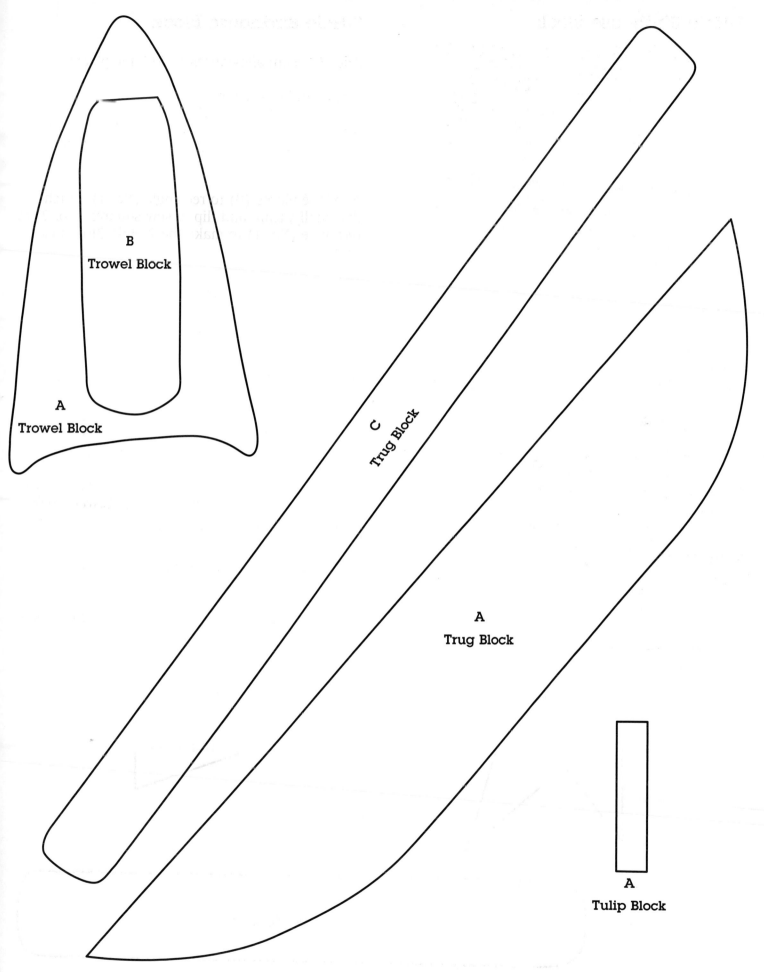

B
Trowel Block

A
Trowel Block

C
Trug Block

A
Trug Block

A
Tulip Block

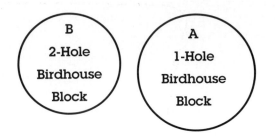

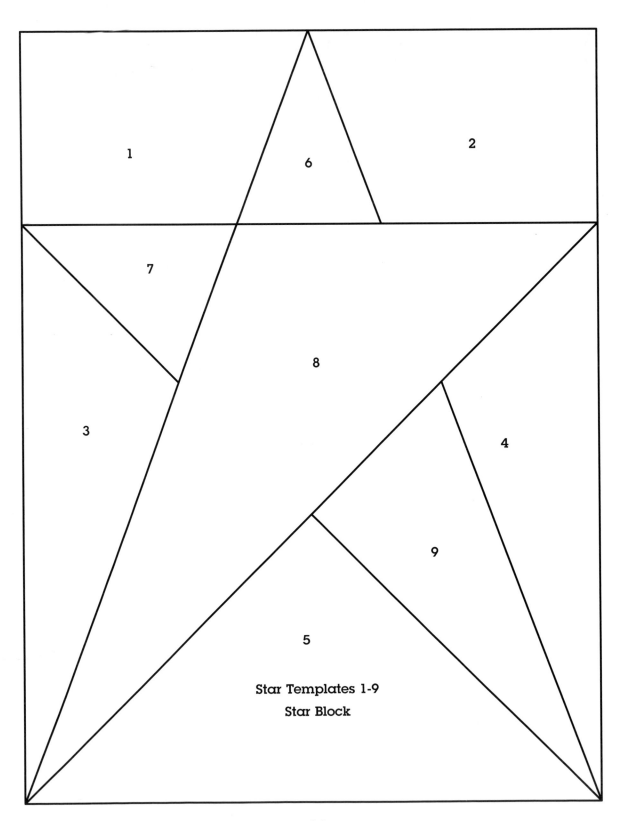

Star Templates 1-9
Star Block

20

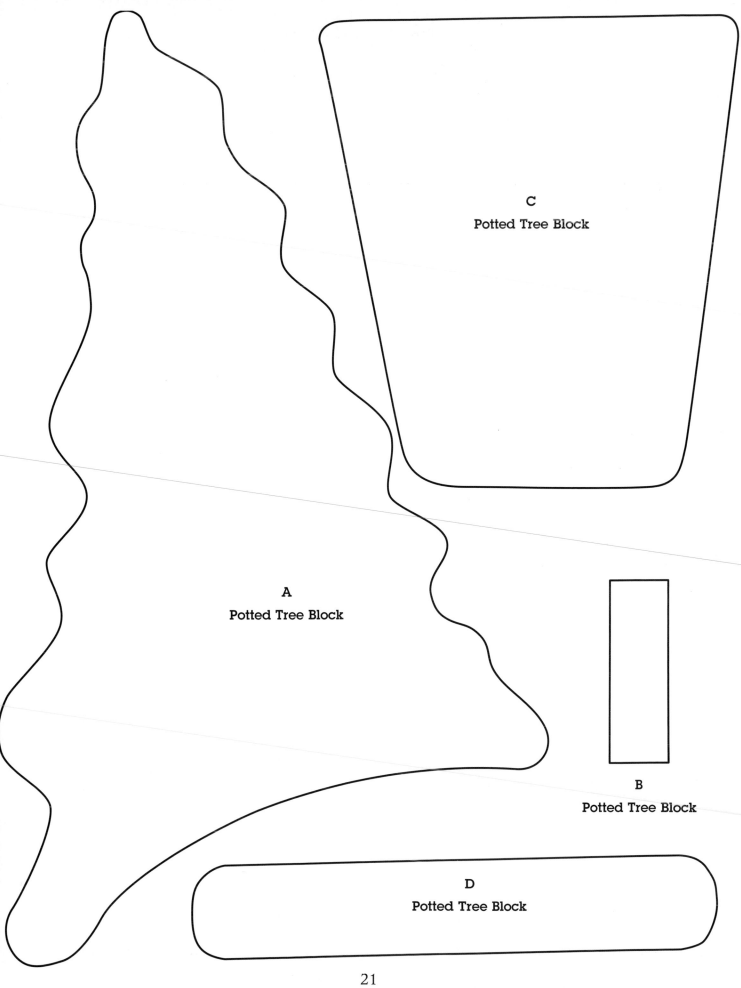

C
Potted Tree Block

A
Potted Tree Block

B
Potted Tree Block

D
Potted Tree Block

5. Blackbirds

Crows and Stars Block

Add ¹/₄" seam allowances to ALL templates.

PIECED STAR BLOCKS
Cutting guide for the 5" Star Block – make 1.

Piece	Color	Cut:
1-5	Tan	1 each from templates 1-5
6-9	Cream	1 each from templates 6-9

Cutting guide for the 7" Star Block – make 1.

Piece	Color	Cut:
1-5	Cream	1 each of templates 1-5
6-9	Tan	1 each of templates 6-9

For each block, refer to the diagram to sew pieces 1-9 together to make the 5" and 7" Star Blocks.

PIECED BACKGROUND
Cutting guide for the pieced background.

Piece	Color	Cut:
No. 1	Cream	1 rectangle 3¹/₂" x 13¹/₂"
No. 2	Cream	1 square 4¹/₂" x 4¹/₂"
No. 3	Cream	1 rectangle 6¹/₂" x 7¹/₂"
No. 4	Cream	1 rectangle 4¹/₂" x 6¹/₂"
No. 5	Cream	1 square 5¹/₂" x 5¹/₂"

Referring to the diagram, sew the star blocks, squares, and rectangles together to make the pieced background.

BRANCHES AND BLACKBIRDS
Cutting guide for the branches and blackbirds.

Piece	Color	Cut:
A	Brown	1 from template A
B	Brown	1 from template B
C	Brown	1 from template C
D	Black	1 and 1 (R) from template D
E	Black	1 and 1 (R) from template E

Referring to the diagram, appliqué the branches and birds onto the pieced background to make the Crows and Stars Block.

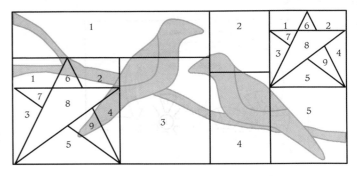

Crows and Stars Pieced Background
Make 1
Finished Size: 10" x 22"

Petunias in a Basket Block

Add ¹/₄" seam allowances to ALL templates.

Cutting guide – make 1.

Piece	Color	Cut:
No. 1	Cream	1 rectangle 10¹/₂" x 12¹/₂"
A	Teal	1 from template A
B	Teal	1 from template B
C	4 Greens	1 each from template C
D	Rose	1 from template D
D	2 Reds	1 each from template D
E	Red	2 from template E
E	Yellow	1 from template E
F	Black	3 from template F

Referring to the diagram for placement, appliqué the basket and flowers onto the cream background rectangle (No. 1).

Referring to the diagram, sew the Crows and Stars Block and the Petunias in a Basket Block together to complete Section 5.

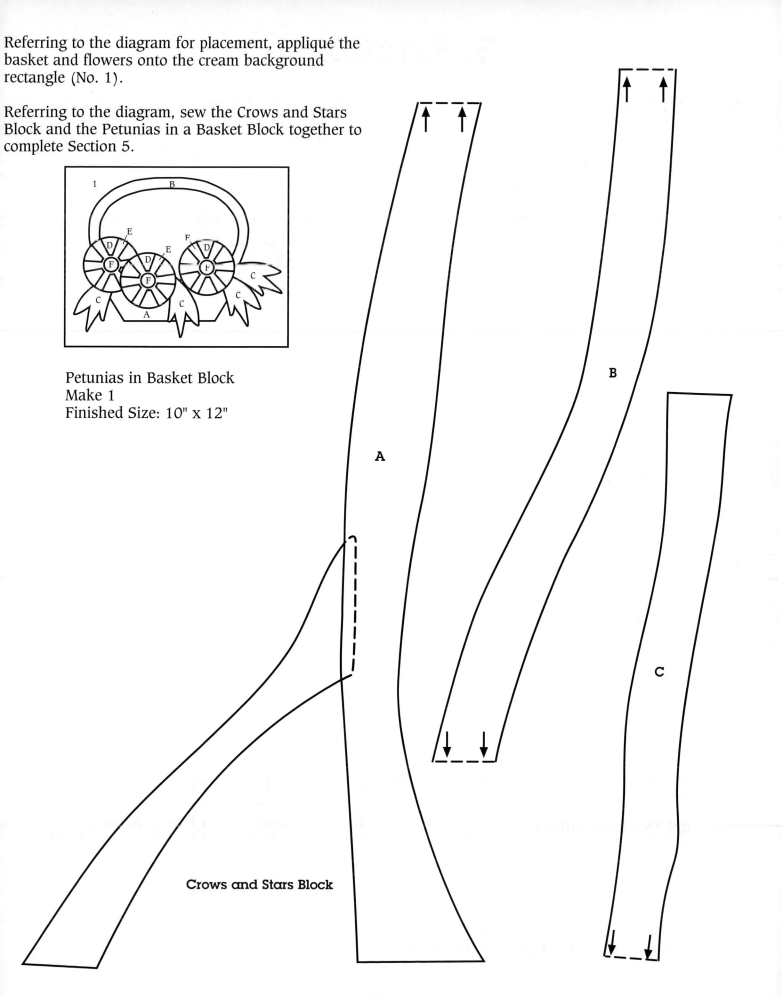

Petunias in Basket Block
Make 1
Finished Size: 10" x 12"

Crows and Stars Block

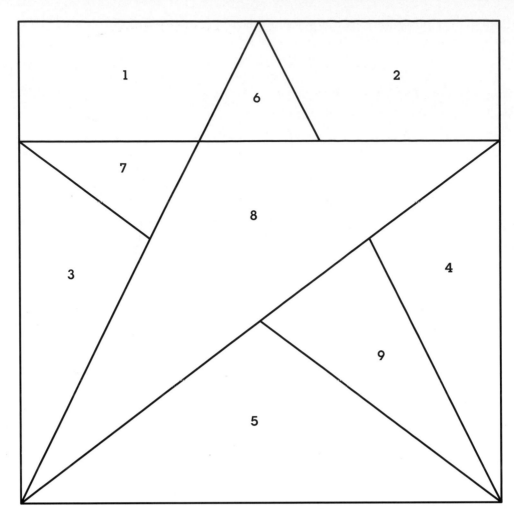

Star Templates 1-9

5" Star Block

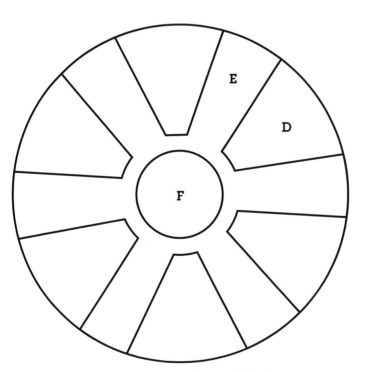

Petunias in a Basket Block

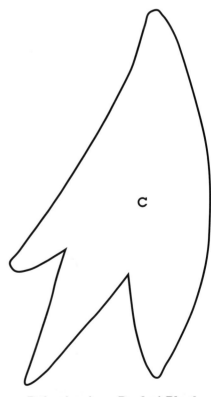

Petunias in a Basket Block

24

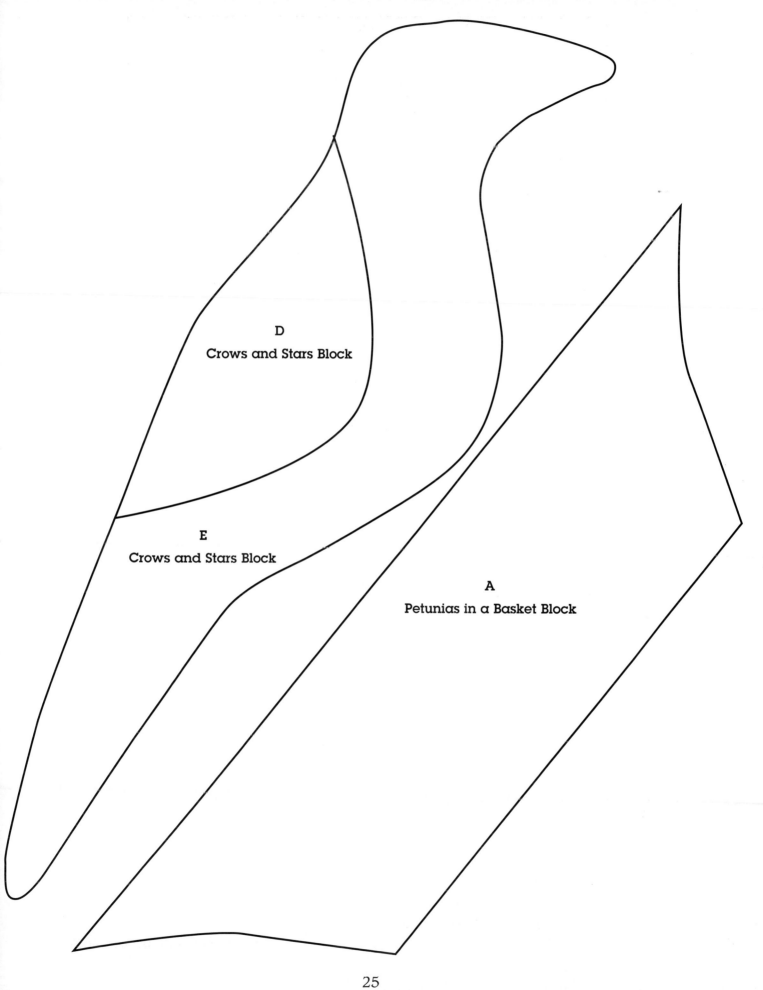

D

Crows and Stars Block

E

Crows and Stars Block

A

Petunias in a Basket Block

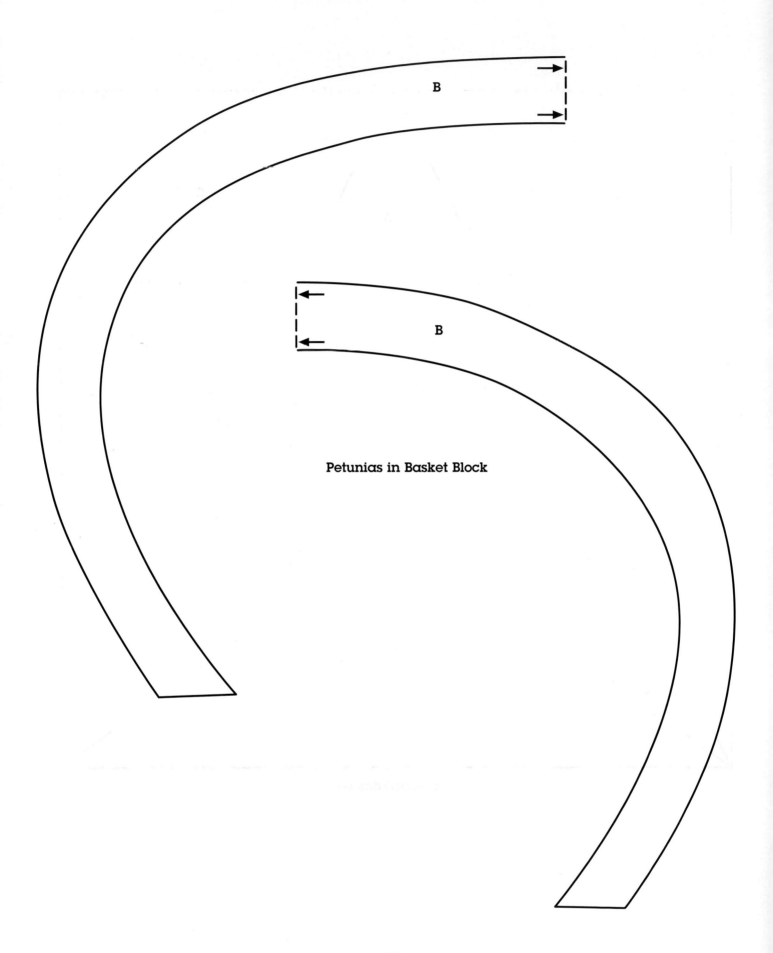

B

B

Petunias in Basket Block

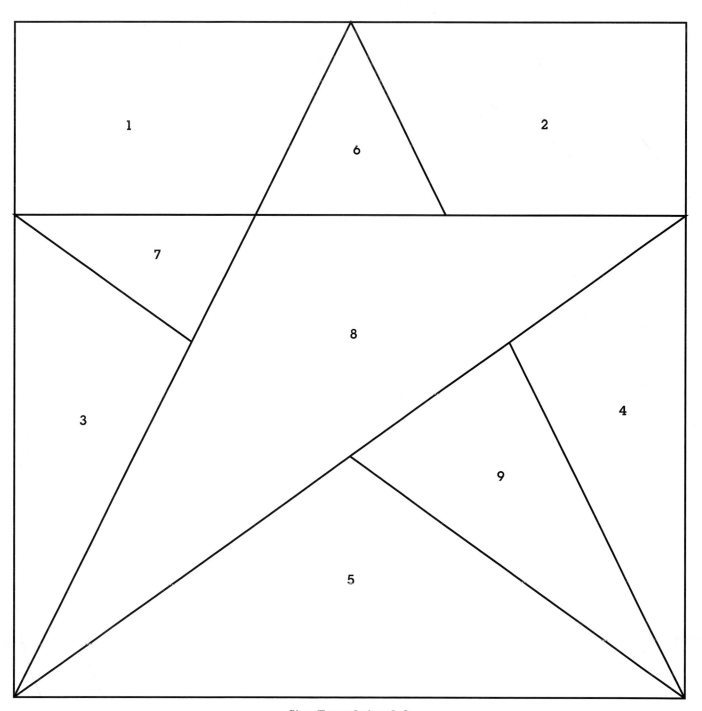

Star Templates 1-9

7" Star Block

6. All-American Garden Chicken!

Small Flag Block

Cutting guide – make 1.

Piece	Color	Cut:
No. 1	Navy	1 rectangle $3^1/_2$" x $5^1/_2$"
No. 2	Red	2 stripes $1^1/_2$" x $9^1/_2$"
No. 3	Cream	1 stripes $1^1/_2$" x $9^1/_2$"
No. 4	Red	2 stripes $1^1/_2$" x $14^1/_2$"
No. 5	Cream	2 stripes $1^1/_2$" x $14^1/_2$"

Referring to the diagram, sew the stripes (Nos. 2-5) and rectangle (No.1) together to make the Small Flag Block.

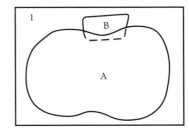

Small Flag Block
Make 1
Finished Size: 7" x 14"

Pumpkin Block

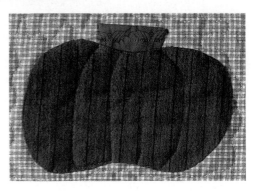

Add $^1/_4$" seam allowances to ALL templates.

Cutting guide – make 1.

Piece	Color	Cut:
No. 1	Blue	1 rectangle $5^1/_2$" x $7^1/_2$"
A	Orange	1 from template A
B	Green	1 from template B

Referring to the diagram for placement, appliqué pieces A and B onto the blue background rectangle (No. 1) to make the Pumpkin Block.

Pumpkin Block
Make 1
Finished Size: 5" x 7"

Carrot Blocks

Add ¹/₄" seam allowances to ALL templates.

Cutting guide for *each* block – make 4.

Piece	Color	Cut:
No. 1	Cream	1 rectangle 1¹/₂" x 3"
No. 2	Orange	1 from template 2
No. 3	Cream	1 and 1(R) from template 3
C	Green	1 from template C

For each block, appliqué piece C onto rectangle (No. 1). Referring to the diagram, sew rectangle and pieces (Nos. 2, 3, and 3R) together to make the Carrot Block.

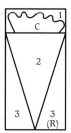

Carrot Block
Make 4
Finished Size: 2¹/₂" x 5"

Sawtooth Star Blocks

Cutting guide for *each* block – make 2.

Piece	Color	Cut:
No. 1	Dark	1 square 3" x 3"
No. 2	Dark	8 squares 1³/₄" x 1³/₄"
No. 3	Light	4 rectangles 1³/₄" x 3"
No. 4	Light	4 squares 1³/₄" x 1³/₄"

For each block, use squares (No. 2) and rectangles (No. 3) to make 4 Flying Geese. Assemble the Flying Geese and the remaining squares to make the Sawtooth Star Block.

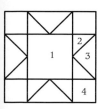

Sawtooth Star Block
Make 2
Finished Size: 5" x 5"

Chicken Block

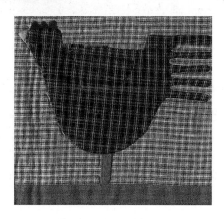

Add ¹/₄" seam allowances to ALL templates.

Cutting guide – make 1.

Piece	Color	Cut:
No. 1	Tan	1 rectangle 8¹/₂" x 10¹/₂"
No. 2	Green	1 rectangle 1¹/₂" x 10¹/₂"
A	Black	1 from template A
B	Red	1 from template B
C	Gold	1 from template C
D	Green	1 from template D

Referring to the diagram, appliqué pieces A-D onto rectangle (No. 1); sew rectangles (Nos. 1 and 2) together to make the Chicken Block.

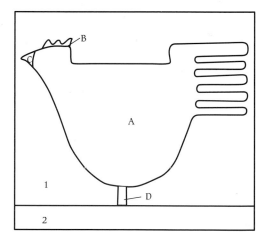

Chicken Block
Make 1
Finished Size: 9" x 10"

Referring to the diagram, sew the Flag and Pumpkin Blocks together. Sew the Carrot Blocks together into pairs, then sew each pair to a Sawtooth Star and sew the two sets together; sew the Chicken Block to the bottom. Sew the two sections together to complete Section 6.

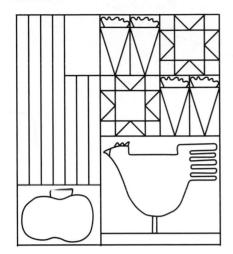

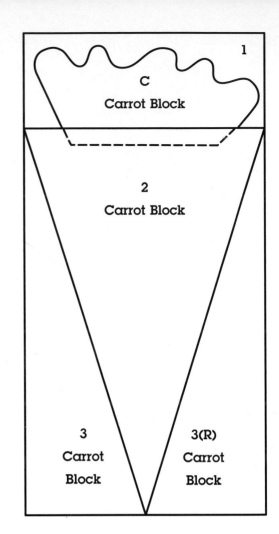

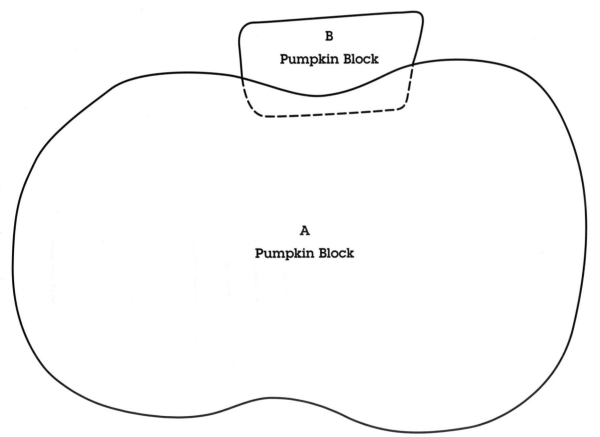

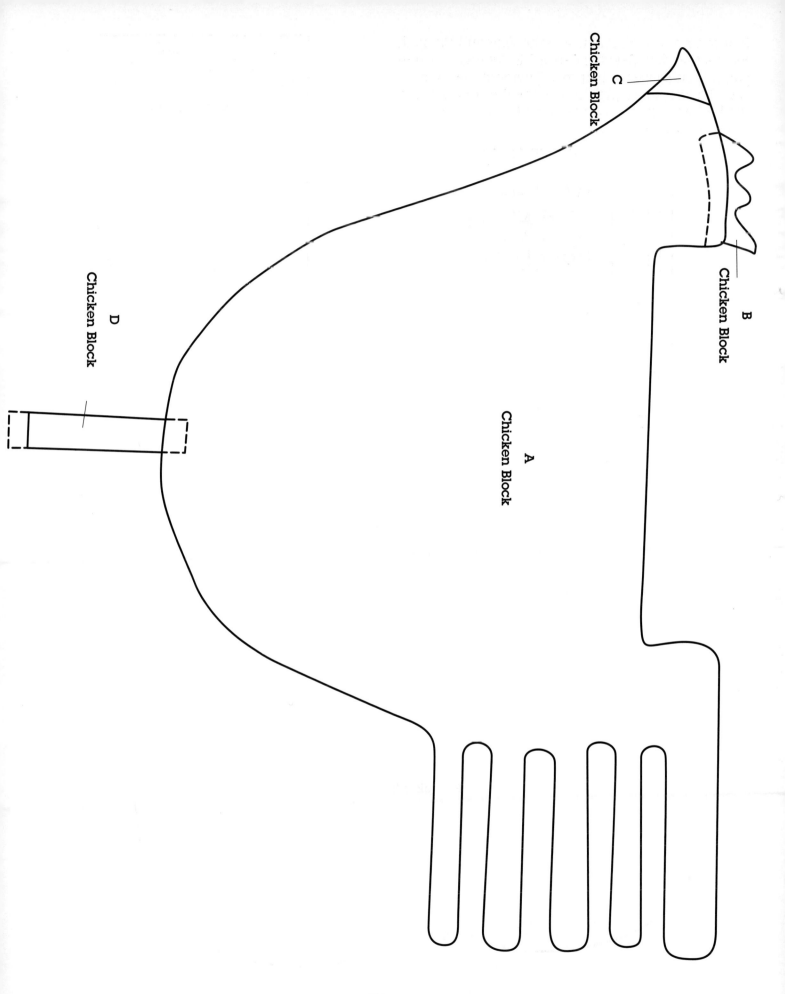

Chicken Block C

Chicken Block B

Chicken Block D

Chicken Block A

7. Yard Art

Chair Block

Referring to the diagram for placement, appliqué piece G to piece A. Appliqué pieces A-F onto the brown background rectangle (No. 1) to make the Chair Block.

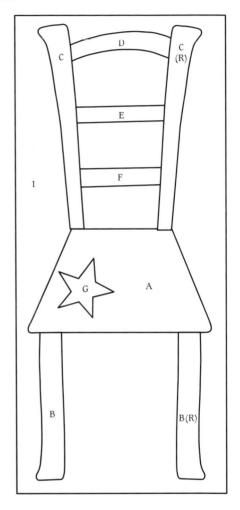

Chair Block
Make 1
Finished Size 8" x 19"

Add $^1/_4$" seam allowances to ALL templates.

Cutting guide – make 1.

Piece	Color	Cut:
No. 1	Brown	1 rectangle $8^1/_2$" x $19^1/_2$"
A	White	1 from template A
B	White	1 and 1(R) from template B
C	White	1 and 1(R) from template C
D	White	1 from template D
E	White	1 from template E
F	White	1 from template F
G	Navy	1 from template G

Beehive Block

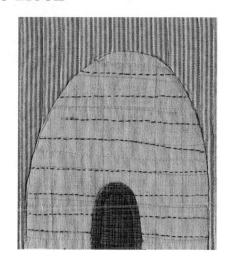

Add ¹/₄" seam allowances to ALL templates.

Cutting guide – make 1.

Piece	Color	Cut:
No. 1	Tan	1 rectangle 7¹/₂" x 8¹/₂"
A	Gold	1 from template A
B	Brown	1 from template B

Referring to the diagram for placement, appliqué piece B onto piece A; appliqué piece A onto tan background rectangle (No. 1) to make Beehive Block. Referring to photo for placement, use 3 strands of brown embroidery floss and a running stitch to work lines across beehive.

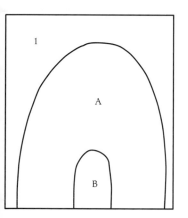

Beehive Block
Make 1
Finished Size: 7" x 8"

Star Block

Add ¹/₄" seam allowances to ALL templates.

Cutting guide – make 1.

Piece	Color	Cut:
1-5	Teal	1 each from templates 1 – 5
6-9	Tan	1 each from templates 6 – 9

Referring to the diagram, sew pieces 1-9 together to make the Star Block.

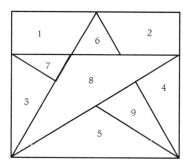

Star Block
Make 1
Finished Size: 6" x 7"

Radish Blocks

Add ¼" seam allowances to ALL templates.

Cutting guide for *each* block – make 2.

Piece	Color	Cut:
No. 1	Blue	1 rectangle 2½" x 3"
A	Red	1 from template A
B	Green	1 from template B

Referring to the diagram for placement, appliqué pieces A and B onto the background rectangle (No. 1) to make each Radish Block.

Radish Block
Make 2
Finished Size: 2" x 2½"

Sawtooth Star Block

Cutting guide – make 1.

Piece	Color	Cut:
No. 1	Blue	1 square 3" x 3"
No. 2	Blue	8 squares 1¾" x 1¾"
No. 3	Tan	4 rectangles 1¾" x 3"
No. 4	Tan	4 squares 1¾" x 1¾"

Referring to the diagram, use squares (No. 2) and rectangles (No. 3) to make 4 Flying Geese. Assemble the Flying Geese and the remaining squares to make the Sawtooth Star Block.

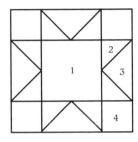

Sawtooth Star Block
Make 1
Finished Size: 5" x 5"

Referring to the diagram, sew the Radish Blocks together; sew them to the Sawtooth Star Block. To these, sew the Star Block, then the Beehive Block. Sew these and the Chair Block together to complete Section 7.

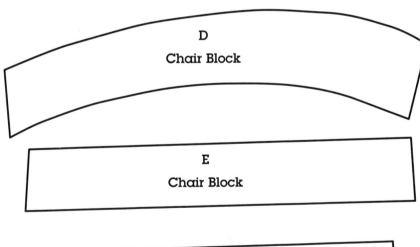

D
Chair Block

E
Chair Block

F
Chair Block

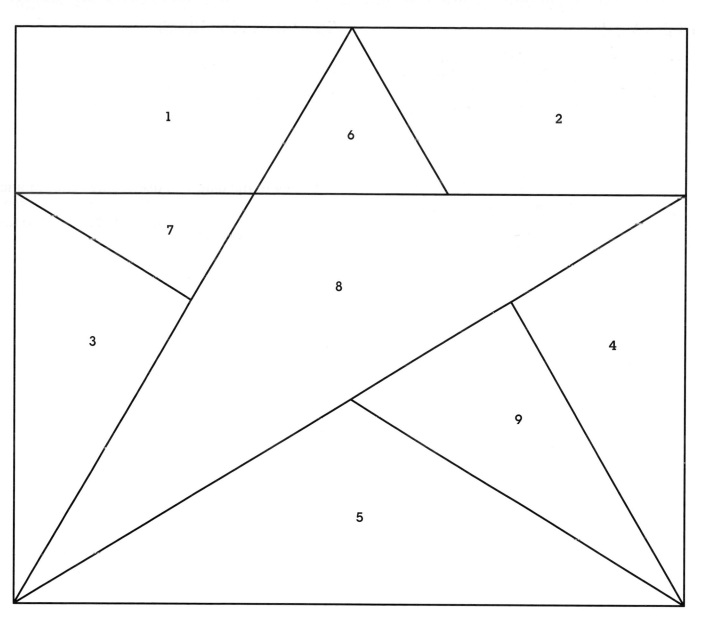

Star Templates 1-9
Star Block

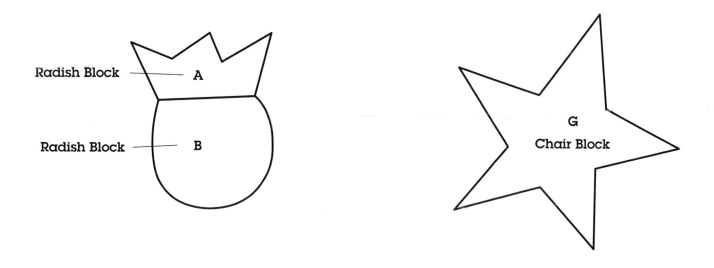

Radish Block —— A

Radish Block —— B

G
Chair Block

35

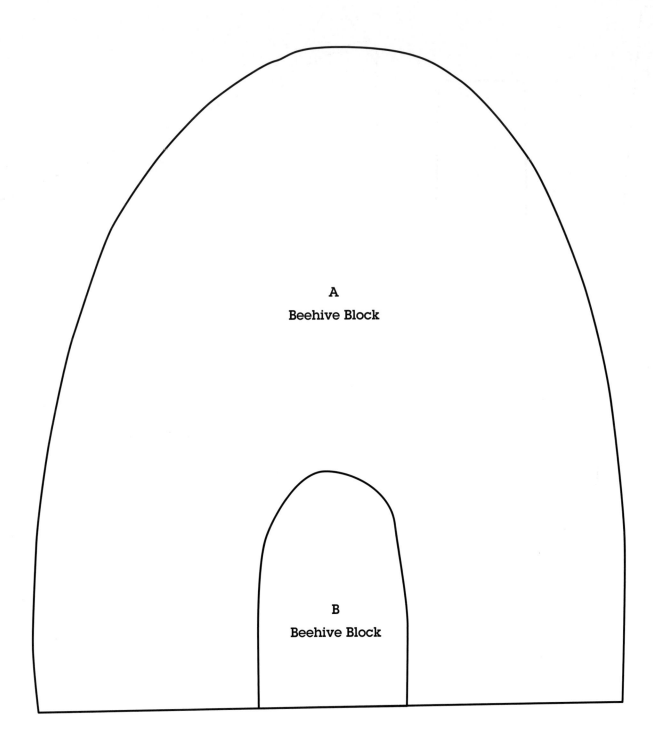

A

Beehive Block

B

Beehive Block

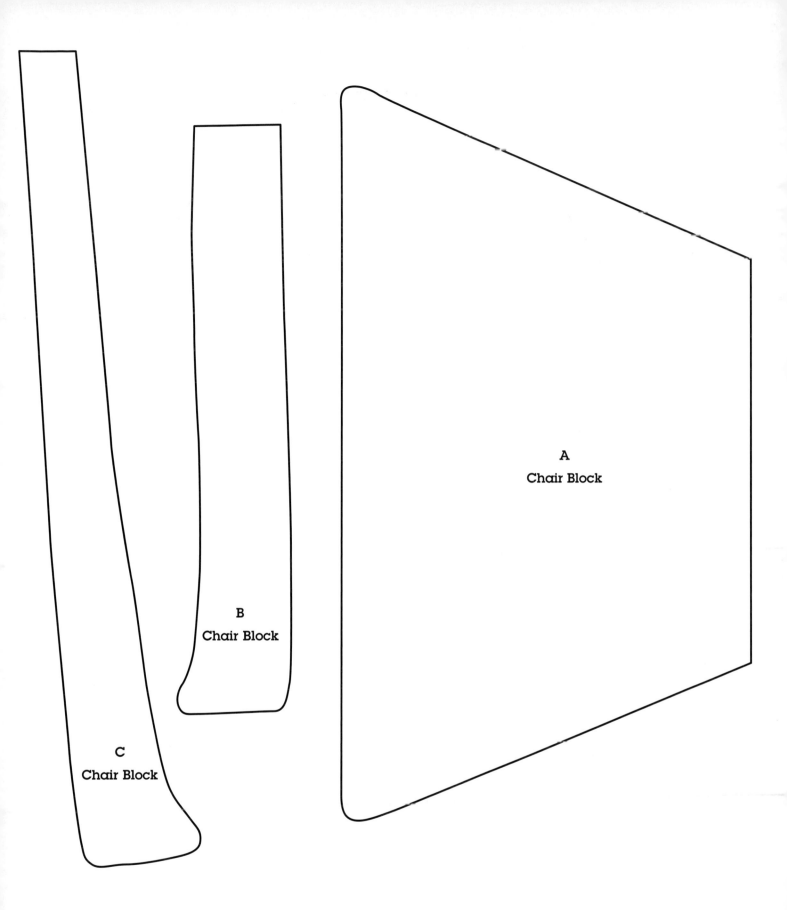

A
Chair Block

B
Chair Block

C
Chair Block

8. Topiaries

Topiary Blocks

The 3 different topiary blocks all have pieced pots using templates and appliquéd green circles and stems. To help identify the blocks, we have named them as follows:

Short Topiary Block (2 circles)
Middle Topiary Block (3 circles)
Tall Topiary Block (3 circles)

SHORT TOPIARY BLOCK

Piece	Color	Cut:
No. 1	Orange	1 rectangle $6^{1}/_{2}$" x $10^{1}/_{2}$"
No. 2	Green	1 rectangle $1^{1}/_{2}$" x $6^{1}/_{2}$"
No. 3	Green	1 from template 3
No. 4	Orange	1 and 1(R) from template 4
A	Green	1 from template A
B	Green	1 from template B
C	Brown	1 from template C
D	Brown	1 from template D

Referring to the diagram for placement, appliqué pieces A-D onto the orange background rectangle (No. 1). Sew pieces 1-4 together to make the Short Topiary Block.

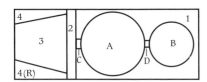

Short Topiary Block
Make 1
Finished Size: 6" x 15"

MIDDLE TOPIARY BLOCK

Piece	Color	Cut:
No. 5	Cream	1 rectangle $5^{1}/_{2}$" x $9^{1}/_{2}$"
No. 6	Orange	1 rectangle $1^{1}/_{4}$" x $5^{1}/_{2}$"
No. 7	Cream	1 rectangle $6^{1}/_{2}$" x $11^{1}/_{2}$"
No. 8	Orange	1 from template 8
No. 9	Cream	1 and 1(R) from tcmplate 9
E	Green	1 from template E
F	Green	2 from template F
G	Brown	3 from template G

Referring to the diagram for placement, appliqué pieces E, one F, and G onto the cream background rectangle (No. 5). Sew rectangles and pieces (Nos. 5-9) together to make the Middle Topiary Block. Sew the Short and Middle Topiary Blocks together; sew rectangle 7 to the Topiary Blocks; appliqué remaining piece F onto the block.

Middle Topiary Block
Make 1
Finished Size: 5" x 15"

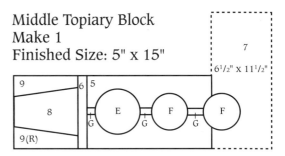

TALL TOPIARY BLOCK

Piece	Color	Cut:
No. 10	Tan	1 rectangle $5^{1}/_{2}$" x $15^{1}/_{2}$"
No. 11	Orange	1 rectangle $1^{3}/_{4}$" x $5^{1}/_{2}$"
No. 12	Orange	1 from template 12
No. 13	Tan	1 and 1(R) from template 13
H	Green	3 from template H
I	Brown	3 from template I

Referring to the diagram for placement, appliqué pieces H and I onto the tan background rectangle (No. 10). Sew rectangles and pieces (Nos. 10-13) together to make the Tall Topiary Block.

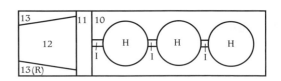

Tall Topiary Block
Make 1
Finished Size: 5" x 21"

Snake Blocks

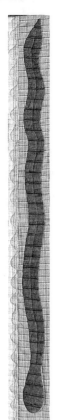

Cutting guide for *each* block – make 2.

Piece	Color	Cut:
No. 1	Light	1 rectangle $4^1/_2$" x $38^1/_2$"
A	Dark	1 from template A

Referring to the diagram for placement, appliqué piece A onto the background rectangle to make each Snake Block. Use 6 strands of black floss to work French knots for eyes.

Note – On our original quilt, a spacer strip was sewn onto each snake block. In these instructions, we have eliminated that extra seam by using a corrected background rectangle measurement.

Referring to the diagram, sew the Tall Topiary Block to the other Topiary Blocks. Sew the Snake Blocks together but do NOT sew them to the Topiary Blocks at this time.

Snake Block
Make 2
Finished Size: 4" x 38"

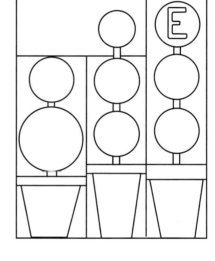

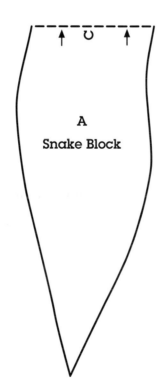

A
Snake Block

C

Short Topiary Block

D-G-I

Short Topiary Block

39

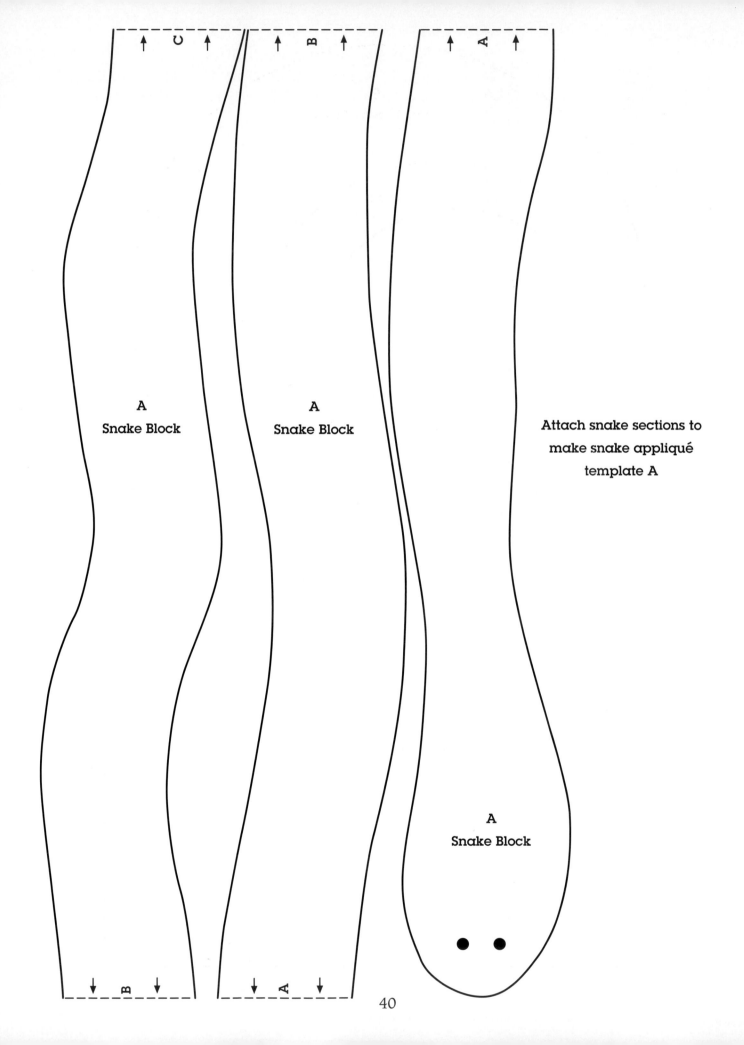

↑ C ↑

A
Snake Block

↑ B ↑

A
Snake Block

↑ A ↑

Attach snake sections to
make snake appliqué
template A

A
Snake Block

↓ B ↓

↓ A ↓

40

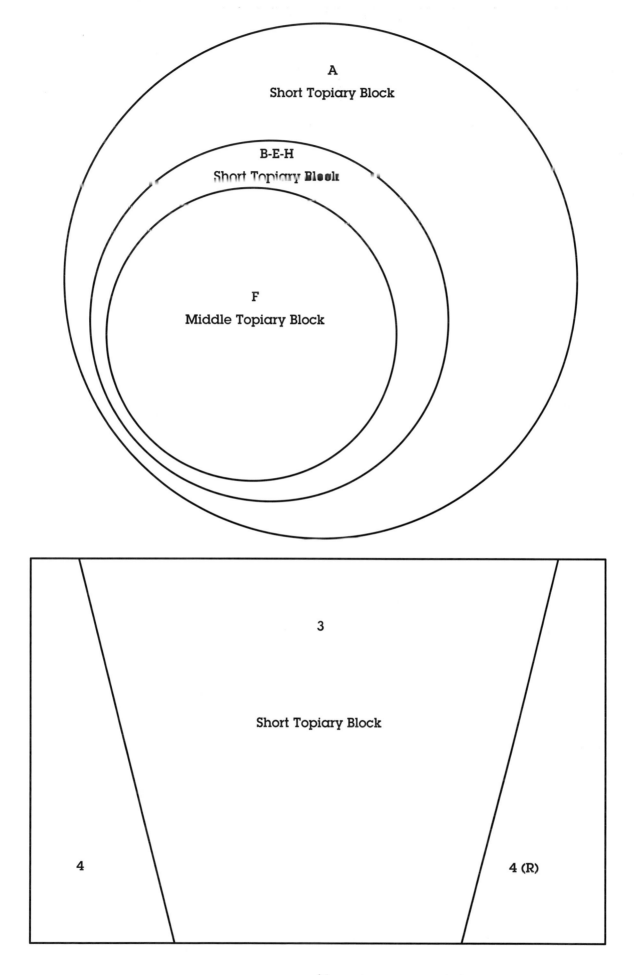

A
Short Topiary Block

B-E-H
Short Topiary Block

F
Middle Topiary Block

3

Short Topiary Block

4

4 (R)

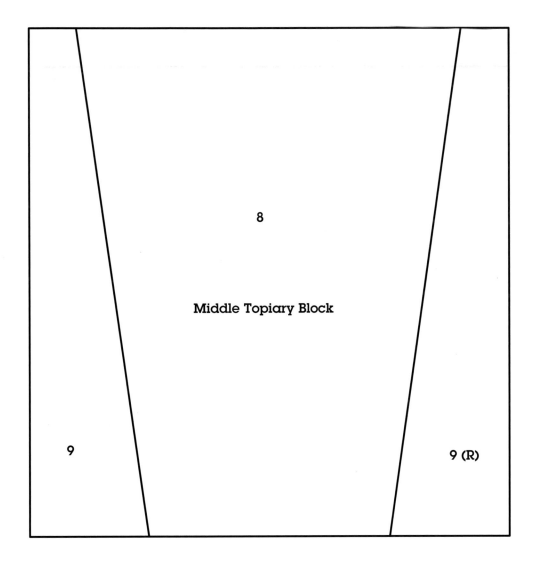

8

Middle Topiary Block

9

9 (R)

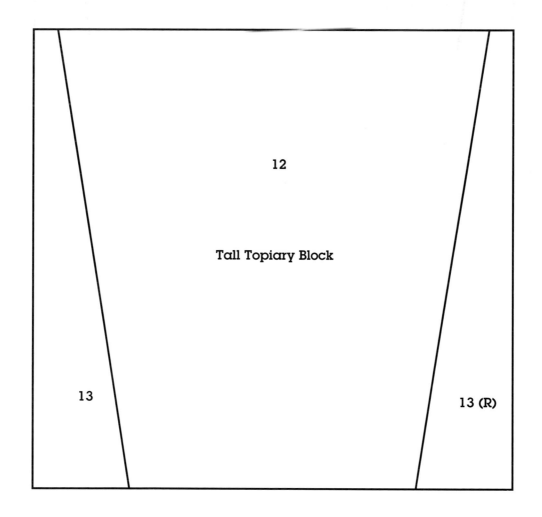

9. Garden Girl

Garden Girl Block

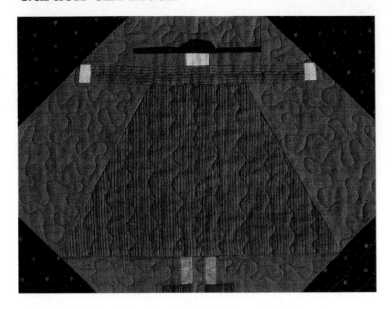

Add $1/4$" seam allowances to ALL templates.

Cutting guide – make 1.

Piece	Color	Cut:
No. 1	Green	1 rectangle 2" x 6"
No. 2	Green	2 rectangles 1" x $2^3/4$"
No. 3	Green	1 square $3^1/8$" x $3^1/8$"
No. 4	Green	1 square $1^5/8$" x $1^5/8$"
No. 5	Green	1 and 1(R) from template 5
No. 6	Green	1 square $2^5/8$" x $2^5/8$"
No. 7	Green	2 rectangles $2^1/4$" x $3^1/4$"
No. 8	Green	2 rectangles $1^1/4$" x $1^3/4$"
No. 9	Green	1 rectangle 1" x $2^1/4$"

No. 10	Orange	1 rectangle $1^1/4$" x $9^1/2$"
No. 11	Orange	1 from template 11
No. 12	Cream	1 rectangle 1" x $1^1/2$"
No. 13	Cream	2 rectangles 1" x $1^1/4$"
No. 14	Maroon	1 rectangle $3/4$" x 6"
A	Maroon	1 from template A
No. 15	Tan	2 rectangles 1" x $1^3/4$"
No. 16	Black	2 rectangles 1" x $1^3/4$"
No. 17	Black	1 square $6^1/8$" x $6^1/8$"
No. 18	Black	1 square $4^5/8$" x $4^5/8$"

Cut each square (Nos. 3, 4, 6, 17, and 18) once diagonally to make 2 triangles. Referring to the diagram, sew the pieces together to make the Garden Girl Block. Appliqué the crown of the hat onto the block.

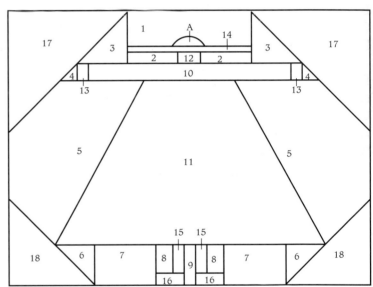

Garden Girl Block
Make 1
Finished Size: 12" x 16"

Birds Block

Add ¹/₄" seam allowances to ALL templates.

Cutting guide – make 1.

Piece	Color	Cut:
No. 1	Tan	1 rectangle 2" x 7"
No. 2	Cream	1 rectangle 5" x 7"
No. 3	Orange	1 rectangle 5" x 10"
No. 4	Tan	1 rectangle 2" x 10"
A	3 Blacks	2 and 1(R) from template A
B	3 Reds	2 and 1(R) from template B
C	3 Creams	2 and 1(R) from template C
D	3 Golds	2 and 1(R) from template D

Referring to the diagram, sew the background rectangles (Nos. 1-4) together. Appliqué pieces A, B, C, and D onto the background to make the Birds Block. Use 6 strands of black embroidery floss to work French knots for eyes.

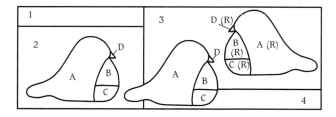

Birds Block
Make 1
Finished Size: 6" x 16"

Checkerboard Spacer

Cutting guide – make 1.

Piece	Color	Cut:
No. 1	Red	16 squares 1¹/₂" x 1¹/₂"
No. 2	Cream	16 squares 1¹/₂" x 1¹/₂"

Referring to the diagram, sew the red and cream squares together into pairs. Sew the 16 pairs together to make the Checkerboard Spacer.

Checkerboard Spacer
Make 1
Finished Size: 2" x 16"

Referring to the diagram, sew the Garden Girl Block, Birds Block, and the Checkerboard Spacer together to complete Section 9.

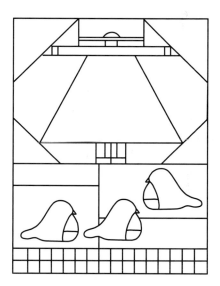

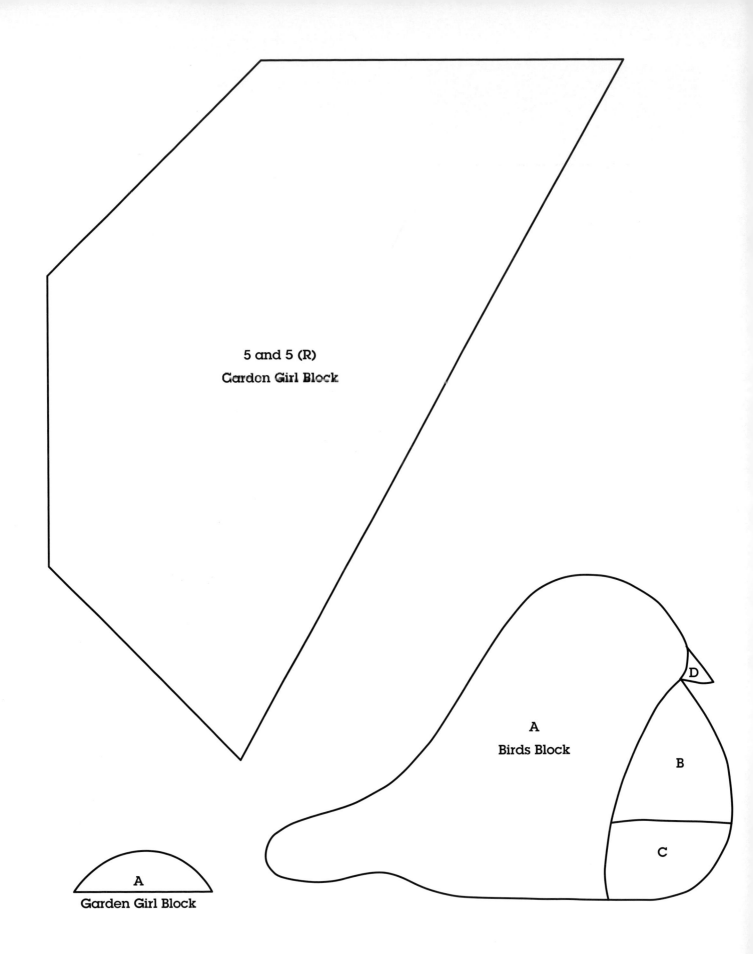

5 and 5 (R)
Garden Girl Block

A
Birds Block

B

D

C

A
Garden Girl Block

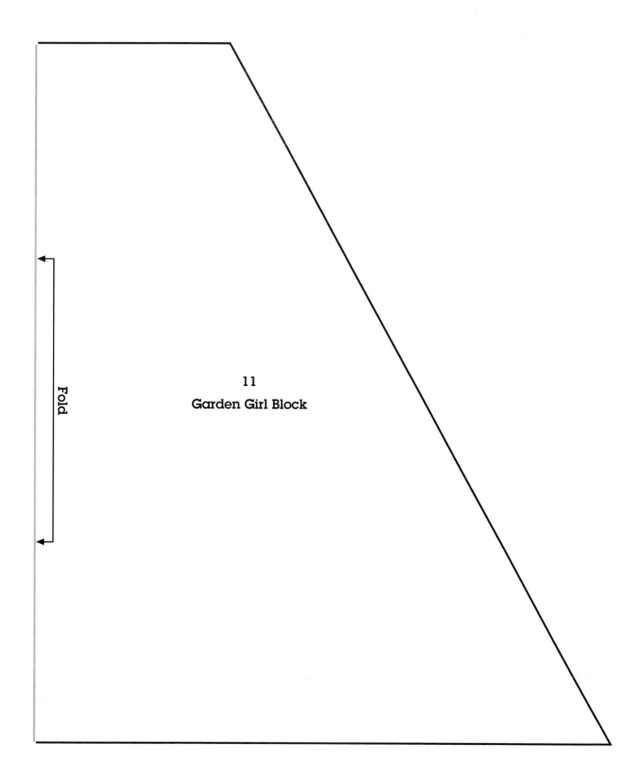

Fold

11
Garden Girl Block

10. Gimme Sunshine

Sun Block

Add ¹/₄" seam allowances to ALL templates.

Cutting guide – make 1.

Piece	Color	Cut:
No. 1	Cream	1 rectangle 6¹/₂" x 28¹/₂"
A	Gold	1 from template A
B	2 Blues	1 each from template B
B	2 Reds	1 each from template B

From an assortment of gold fabrics, cut 70 squares 2" x 2".

To make the paper-pieced sun:
1. Sew 50 gold squares together into pairs. Sew five pairs together to make five 4-square units. Sew one square to 14 of the remaining pairs to make 3-square units.
2. Use the pattern given to cut a foundation for the patchwork sun from newsprint or freezer paper.

3. Starting at the center of the paper foundation and working toward each end, use the sew-and-flip method to sew the gold square units to the foundation. Off-set the units so that the seams don't line up and vary the angle of the units and the seam allowances for a random look. Make sure the piecing extends at least ¹/₂" beyond all edges of the paper foundation.
4. Stay stitch just outside the edge of the foundation. Carefully tear away the paper foundation; trim fabric ¹/₄" from stay stitching line.
5. Referring to the diagram, position the pieced sun on the background rectangle (No. 1) and baste in place. Appliqué piece A onto the background at the top of the pieced sun. Appliqué the 4 stars in place to make the Sun Block and complete Section 10.

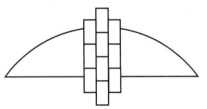

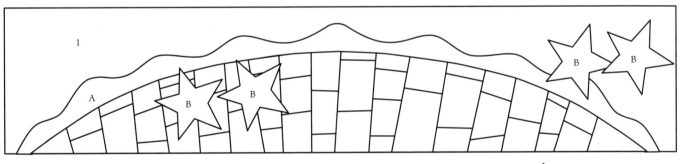

Sun Block
Make 1
Finished Size: 6" x 28"

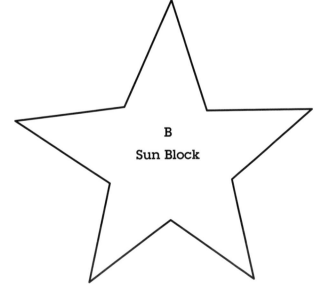

B
Sun Block

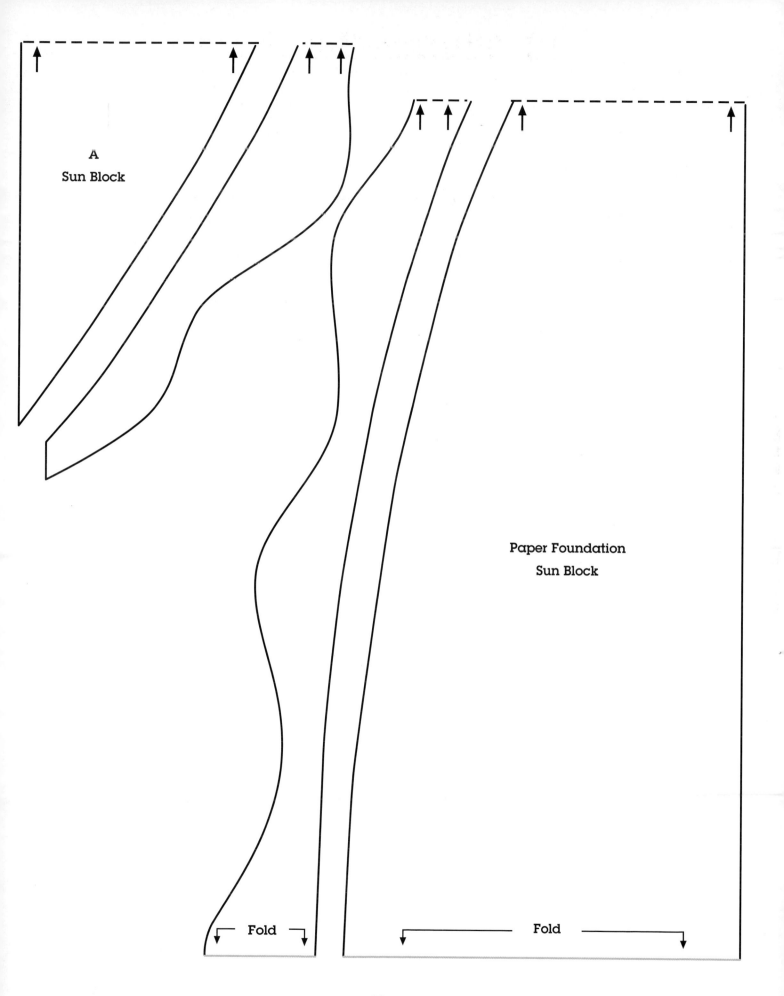

A
Sun Block

Paper Foundation
Sun Block

Fold

Fold

49

11. Sunflower

Sunflower Block

The sunflower block uses two different piecing techniques. The 2 circles and the star are appliquéd; the outer circle is paper pieced. Complete instructions follow the cutting guide.

Add $^1/_4$" seam allowances to ALL templates.

Cutting guide – make 1.

Piece	Color	Cut:
No. 1	Cream	1 strip $2^1/_2$" x 45"
No. 2	Blue	1 strip $2^1/_2$" x 45"
No. 7	Tan	1 square $12^1/_2$" x $12^1/_2$"
A	Teal	1 from template A
B	Rust	1 from template B
C	Gold	1 from template C

To make the paper-pieced circle:
1. Use the pattern given to cut 4 paper foundations. Beginning with cream and ending with blue, use the sew-and-flip method to piece each foundation. Make sure the piecing extends at least $^1/_2$" beyond all edges of the paper foundation.
2. Stay stitch just outside the edge of the foundation. Sew the 4 units together to form a circle. Carefully tear away the paper foundations; trim fabric $^1/_4$" from stay stitching line.

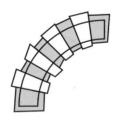 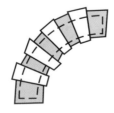

3. Position the pieced circle on the background square (No. 7). Appliqué the outer edge only to the background. Appliqué pieces A, B, and C in place, trimming away the fabric behind each appliqué, to make the Sunflower Block.

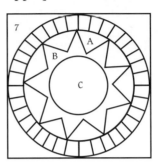

Sunflower Block
Make 1
Finished Size: 12" x 12

Background

Cutting guide – make 1.

Piece	Color	Cut:
No. 1	Cream	1 rectangle $5^1/_2$" x $9^1/_2$"
No. 2	Tan	1 rectangle $5^1/_2$" x $9^1/_2$"
No. 3	Cream	1 rectangle $3^1/_2$" x $10^1/_2$"
No. 4	Tan	1 rectangle $4^1/_2$" x $12^1/_2$"
No. 5	Tan	1 rectangle $3^1/_2$" x $4^1/_2$"
No. 6	Cream	1 rectangle $3^1/_2$" x $8^1/_2$"
No. 8	Tan	1 rectangle $7^1/_2$" x $12^1/_2$"
No. 9	Tan	1 rectangle $5^1/_2$" x $8^1/_2$"
No. 10	Cream	1 rectangle $4^1/_2$" x $5^1/_2$"

Referring to the diagram, sew the rectangles and the Sunflower Block together to complete Section 11.

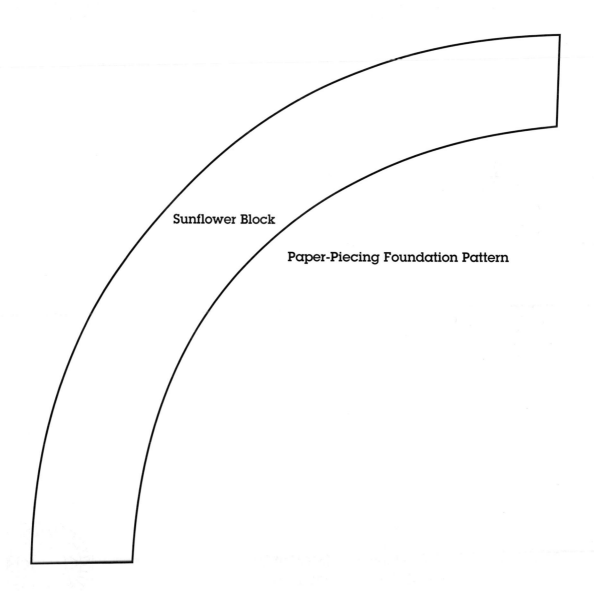

Sunflower Block

Paper-Piecing Foundation Pattern

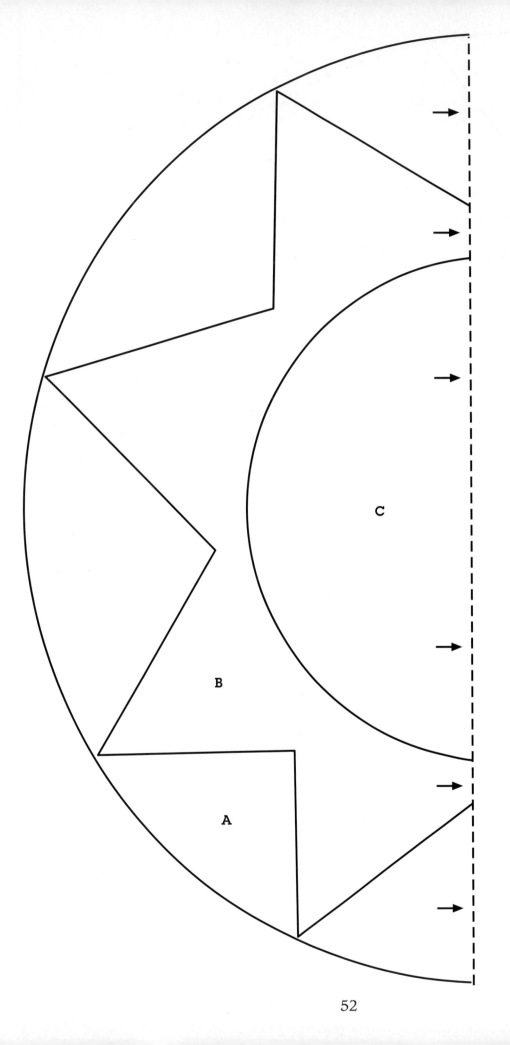

C

B

A

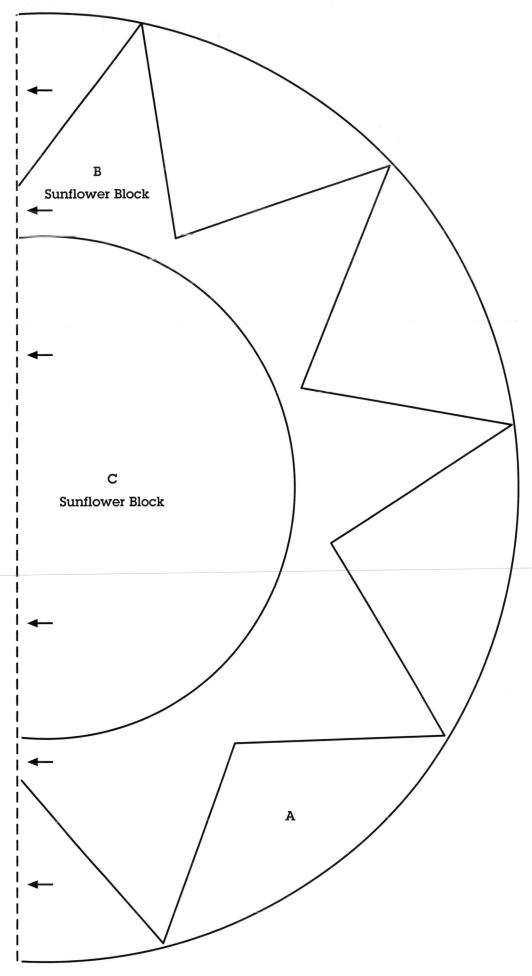

B
Sunflower Block

C
Sunflower Block

A

53

12. Birdhouse Gourds and Favorite Tools

Birdhouse Gourds Block

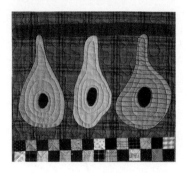

Add ¹/₄" seam allowances to ALL templates.

Cutting guide – make 1.

Piece	Color	Cut:
No. 1	Brown	1 rectangle 11¹/₂" x 14¹/₂"
A	Cream	1 from template A
B	Cream	1 from template B
C	Cream	1 from template C
D	Brown	1 from template D
E	Brown	1 from template E
F	Brown	1 from template F

Referring to the diagram, appliqué pieces D-F to pieces A-C. Appliqué pieces A-C to the brown background rectangle (No. 1), leaving the top portion of each piece unattached until after the shovel handle (A) has been stitched in place.

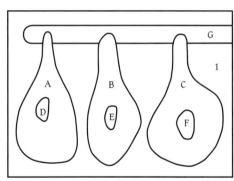

Birdhouse Gourds Block
Make 1
Finished Size: 11" x 14"

Checkerboard Spacer

Cutting guide – make 1.

Piece	Color	Cut:
No. 1	Red	14 squares 1¹/₂" x 1¹/₂"
No. 2	Cream	14 squares 1¹/₂" x 1¹/₂"

Sew red and cream squares together into pairs. Sew the 14 pairs together into a row to make the Checkerboard Spacer.

Checkerboard Spacer
Make 1
Finished Size: 2" x 14"

Quilt Top Assembly

Referring to the diagram, sew Sections 1 though 12 together to make the quilt top. *Note* – There will be some set-in seams.

Shovel

Add ¹/₄" seam allowances to ALL templates.

Cutting guide – make 1.

Piece	Color	Cut:
G	Brown	1 from template G
H	Brown	1 from template H
I	Green	1 from template I

Referring to the diagram, appliqué the shovel pieces (G-I) onto the quilt top.

Rake

Cutting guide – make 1.

Piece	Color	Cut:
J	Blue	1 from template J
K	Rust	1 from template K
L	Brown	1 from template L
M	Brown	9 from template M

Referring to the diagram, appliqué the rake pieces (J-M) onto the quilt top.

Small Tools

Cutting guide.

Piece	Color	Cut:
N	Tan	1 from template N
O	Blue	1 from template O
P	Brown	1 from template P
Q	Gold	1 from template Q
R	Rust	1 from template R
S	Red	1 from template S
T	Teal	1 from template T
U	Tan	1 from template U

Referring to the diagram, appliqué the small tool pieces (N-U) onto the Sunflower Block.

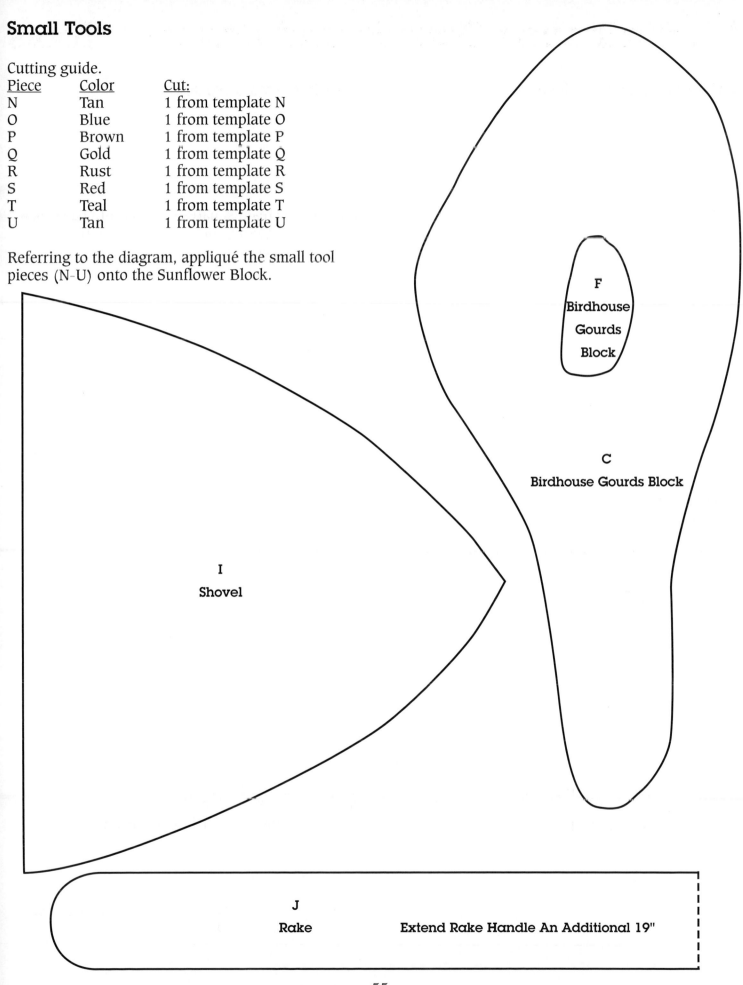

F
Birdhouse
Gourds
Block

C
Birdhouse Gourds Block

I
Shovel

J

Rake   Extend Rake Handle An Additional 19"

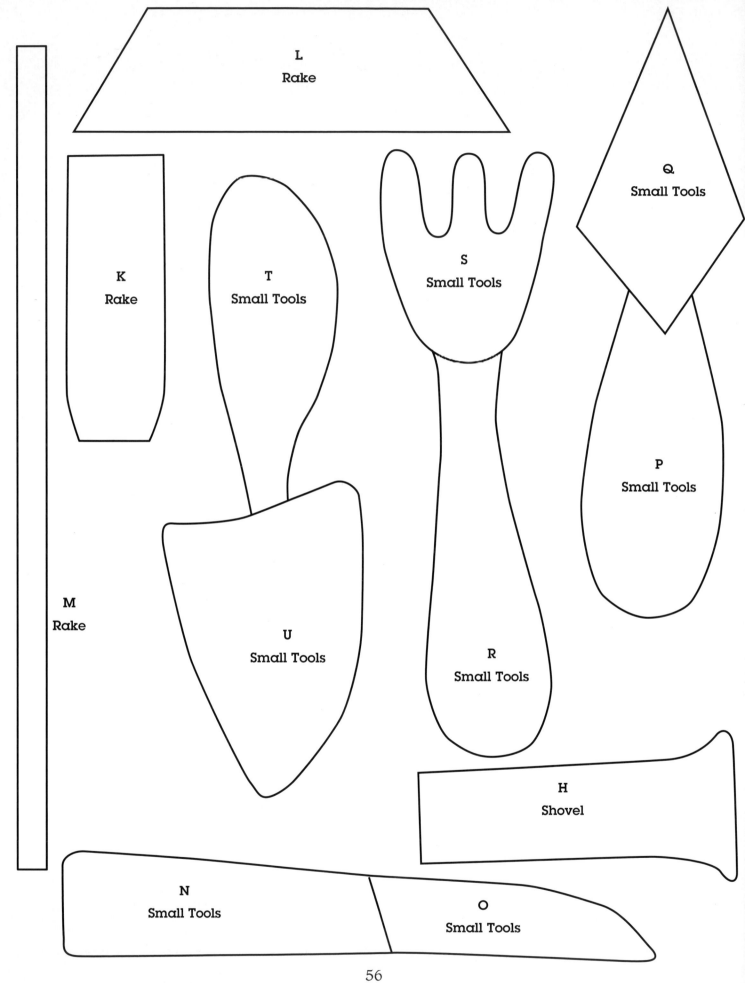

L
Rake

Q
Small Tools

K
Rake

T
Small Tools

S
Small Tools

M
Rake

P
Small Tools

U
Small Tools

R
Small Tools

H
Shovel

N
Small Tools

O
Small Tools

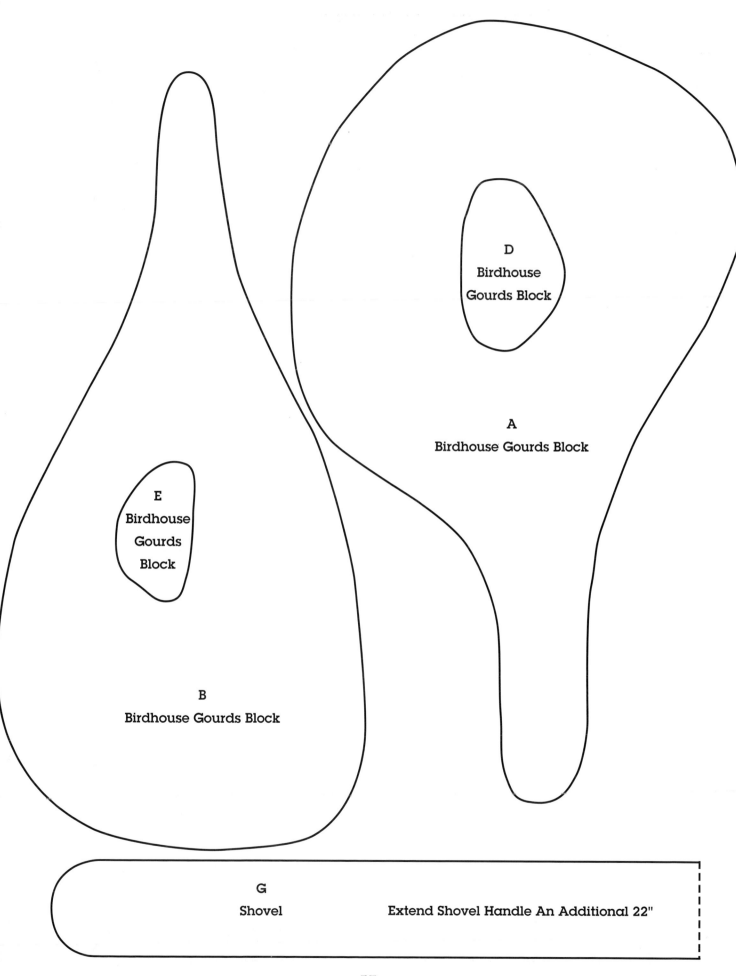

D
Birdhouse
Gourds Block

A
Birdhouse Gourds Block

E
Birdhouse
Gourds
Block

B
Birdhouse Gourds Block

G
Shovel   Extend Shovel Handle An Additional 22"

13. Garden Borders

Top Border (North)

Cutting guide – make 1.

Piece	Color	Cut:
No. 1	Assorted	8 squares $4^{1}/_{2}$" x $4^{1}/_{2}$"
No. 2	Assorted	6 squares $4^{7}/_{8}$" x $4^{7}/_{8}$"

Cut squares (No. 2) once diagonally to make 12 triangles. Sew the triangles together to make 6 triangle-squares. Referring to the diagram, sew the triangle-squares and the squares (No. 1) together into a row to make the Top Border. Sew the Top Border to the quilt top.

Bottom Border (South)

Cutting guide – make 1.

Piece	Color	Cut:
No. 1	Assorted	8 squares $4^{1}/_{2}$" x $4^{1}/_{2}$"
No. 2	Assorted	6 squares $3^{3}/_{8}$" x $3^{3}/_{8}$"
No. 3	Assorted	12 squares $2^{7}/_{8}$" x $2^{7}/_{8}$"

Cut the squares (No. 3) once diagonally to make 24 triangles. Sew one triangle to each side of square (No. 2) to make 6 Square-in-a-Square Blocks. Referring to the diagram, sew the Square-in-a-Square Blocks and the squares (No. 1) together to make the Bottom Border. Sew the Bottom Border to the quilt top.

Right Border (East)

Cutting guide – make 1.

Piece	Color	Cut:
No. 1	Dark	21 squares $4^{1}/_{2}$" x $4^{1}/_{2}$"

Referring to the diagram, sew the squares together into a row to make the Right Border. Sew the Right Border to the quilt top.

Left Border (West)

Cutting guide – make 1.

Piece	Color	Cut:
No. 1	Light	36 rectangles $2^{1}/_{2}$" x $4^{1}/_{2}$"
No. 2	Dark	72 squares $2^{1}/_{2}$" x $2^{1}/_{2}$"
No. 3	Dark	3 squares $4^{1}/_{2}$" x $4^{1}/_{2}$"

Sew the squares (No. 2) to the rectangles (No. 1) to make the 36 Flying Geese Blocks. Referring to the diagram, sew the Flying Geese Blocks and the squares (No. 3) together into a row to make the Left Border. Sew the Left Border to the quilt top.

Letters

Add $^{1}/_{4}$" seam allowances to ALL templates.

Cutting guide – make 1.

Piece	Color	Cut:
N	Green	1 from template N
S	Rust	1 from template S
E	Brown	1 from template E
W	Green	1 from template W

Referring to the diagram, appliqué the letters in place to complete the quilt top.

Finishing the Quilt

Layer the quilt top, batting, and backing and quilt as desired. Use $2^{1}/_{2}$" wide bias strips to bind the quilt with double-fold binding. Label the quilt.

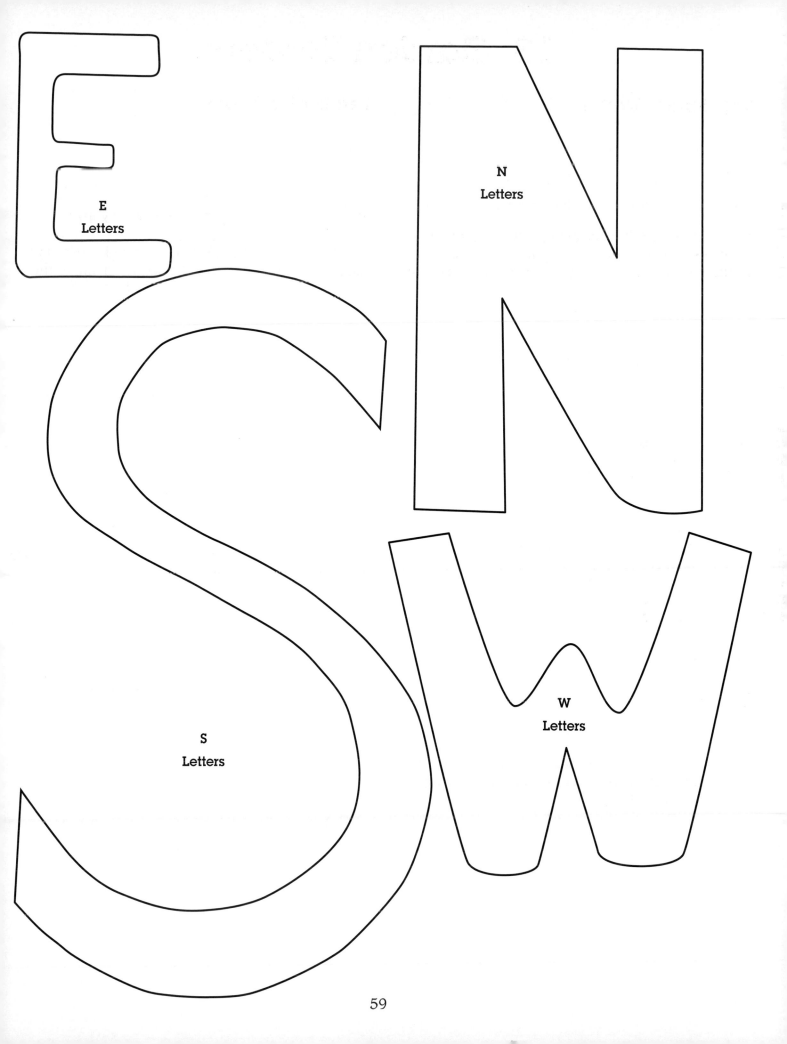

E
Letters

N
Letters

S
Letters

W
Letters

59

Assembly Diagram

Every Bloomin' Thing

Flying geese encircle a wreath of country blossoms and gardening tools on this cozy little quilt. All triangles and squares, the piecing is a breeze. A quilter with moderate sewing skills will have no problem stitching the appliqué shapes as well. Ideal as a lap quilt or a wallhanging, this project can also be used as a table topper!

Since this is a medallion quilt, the cutting directions for each border are given separately. Please refer to the color photo for color choices and fabric selections. The finished quilt measures 36" x 36".

Center Block

Add ¼" seam allowances to ALL templates.

Cutting guide – make 1.

Piece	Color	Cut:
No. 1	Assorted	9 squares 4½" x 4½"
A	Assorted	4 from template A
B	Assorted	4 from template B
C	Assorted	4 from template C
D	Assorted	4 from template D

The following templates are on page 56:

N – U	Assorted	1 each from templates N - U

Sew the squares (No. 1) together in 3 rows of 3, then sew the rows together to make a 9-Patch Block. Cut a 40" length of 1½"w bias strip, piecing if necessary. With wrong sides together, fold the strip in half and sew a ¼" seam along the entire length of the strip. Position the seam at the back of the vine strip. Referring to the diagram, arrange the vine on the block and appliqué in place. Appliqué pieces A-D (from patterns on this page) and pieces N-U (from page 56) in place over the vine to complete the Center Block.

First Border

Cutting guide.

Piece	Color	Cut:
No. 2	Darks	24 rectangles 2½" x 4½"
No. 3	Lights	48 squares 2½" x 2½"
No. 4	Golds	4 squares 4½" x 4½"

Use rectangles (No. 2) and squares (No. 3) to make 24 flying geese. Sew 6 flying geese together to make a flying geese border; repeat to make 4 borders. Sew one flying geese border each to two opposite sides of the center block. Sew one square (No. 4) to each end of each remaining flying geese border; sew one border to each remaining side of center block.

Second Border

Cutting guide.

Piece	Color	Cut:
No. 5	Light	12 squares 4⅞" x 4⅞"
No. 6	Dark	12 squares 4⅞" x 4⅞"

Cut each square (Nos. 5 and 6) once diagonally to make a total of 48 triangles. Sew light and dark triangles together in pairs to make 24 triangle-squares. Sew 5 triangle-squares together to make each side border and 7 triangle-squares each together to make top and bottom borders. Sew the side borders, then the top and bottom borders to the center block.

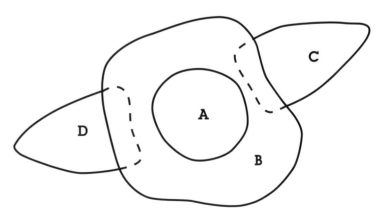

Third Border

Cutting guide.

Piece	Color	Cut:
No. 7	Dark	28 squares 4$\frac{1}{2}$" x 4$\frac{1}{2}$"
No. 8	Dark	4 squares 4$\frac{1}{2}$" x 4$\frac{1}{2}$"
No. 9	Light	16 squares 2$\frac{1}{2}$" x 2$\frac{1}{2}$"

Sew 7 squares (No. 7) together to make one border; repeat to make a total of four borders. Sew two of the borders to opposite sides of the center block. Use squares (Nos. 8 and 9) to make 4 Square-in-a-Square Blocks; sew one block to each end of each remaining border; sew borders to remaining edges of center block.

Finishing the Quilt

Layer the quilt top, batting, and backing and quilt as desired. Use 2$\frac{1}{2}$" wide bias strips to bind the quilt with double-fold binding. Label the quilt.

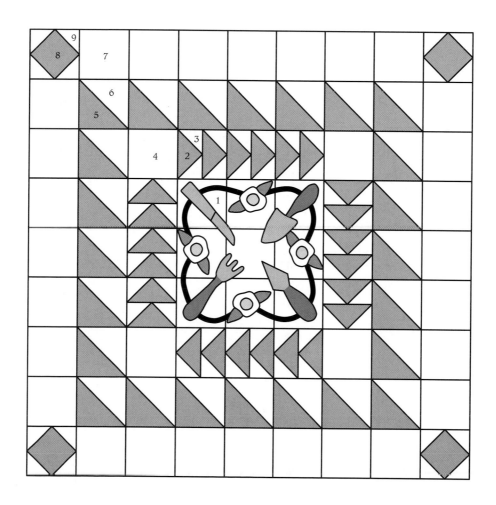

A Cozy Afternoon

Wherever you like to settle in with your cup of tea, coffee, or cocoa, you can add country warmth to your surroundings with this table set. Piece a quick trio of homespun stars for each place mat, and appliqué a basket of flowers for the tea cozy. Just see if that favorite beverage doesn't taste better now!

Tea Cozy

Add $1/4$" seam allowances to ALL templates and use a $1/4$" seam allowance for all sewing.

Use the Tea Cozy pattern to cut 2 pieces each from tan fabric, lining fabric, and batting. Referring to the cutting guide for the Petunias in a Basket Block, page 22, use the patterns for templates A through F to cut out the appliqué pieces for the basket and flowers; appliqué to the tea cozy front.

Place the tea cozy front and lining pieces right sides together; place a batting piece on the wrong side of the tea cozy front. Stitch the pieces together along the straight bottom edge only; fold the lining piece down and press. Repeat with the tea cozy back. Place the front and back pieces right sides together. Leaving an opening for turning, stitch along outside edge. Turn the tea cozy right side out and sew the opening closed. Fold the lining to the inside.

Tea Cozy Assembly Diagram

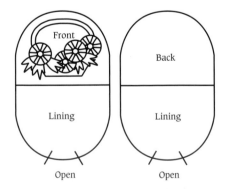

Place Mat

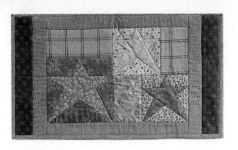

Add $1/4$" seam allowances to ALL templates.

Cutting guide for *each* place mat – make 2.

Piece	Color	Cut;
No. 1	Tan	1 rectangle $3^{1}/2$" x $7^{1}/2$"
No. 2	Tan	2 rectangles $3^{1}/2$" x $5^{1}/2$"
No. 3	Tan	2 rectangles 2" x $15^{1}/2$"
No. 4	Tan	2 rectangles 2" x $13^{1}/2$"
No. 5	Orange	2 rectangles $2^{1}/2$" x $13^{1}/2$"
No. 6	Tan	1 mat backing $13^{1}/2$" x $22^{1}/2$"
No. 7	Batting	1 rectangle $13^{1}/2$" x $22^{1}/2$"

5" STAR BLOCK
Cutting guide for *each* block – make 2.
Use templates 1-9 for 5" Star Block, page 24.

Piece	Color	Cut:
1-5	Medium	Cut 1 each from templates 1-5
6-9	Light	Cut 1 each from templates 6-9

7" STAR BLOCK
Cutting guide – make 1.
Use templates 1-9 for 7" Star Block, page 27.

Piece	Color	Cut:
1-5	Light	Cut 1 each from templates 1-5
6-9	Medium	Cut 1 each from templates 6-9

Referring to the diagram, use rectangles (Nos. 1-5) and Star Blocks to piece each place mat top. Place place mat top and backing right sides together; place the batting piece on the wrong side of place mat top. Leaving an opening for turning, stitch along outside edges. Trim corners, turn the place mat right side out and sew the opening closed.

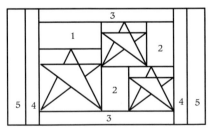

Place Mat Assembly Diagram
Finished Size: 13" x 22"

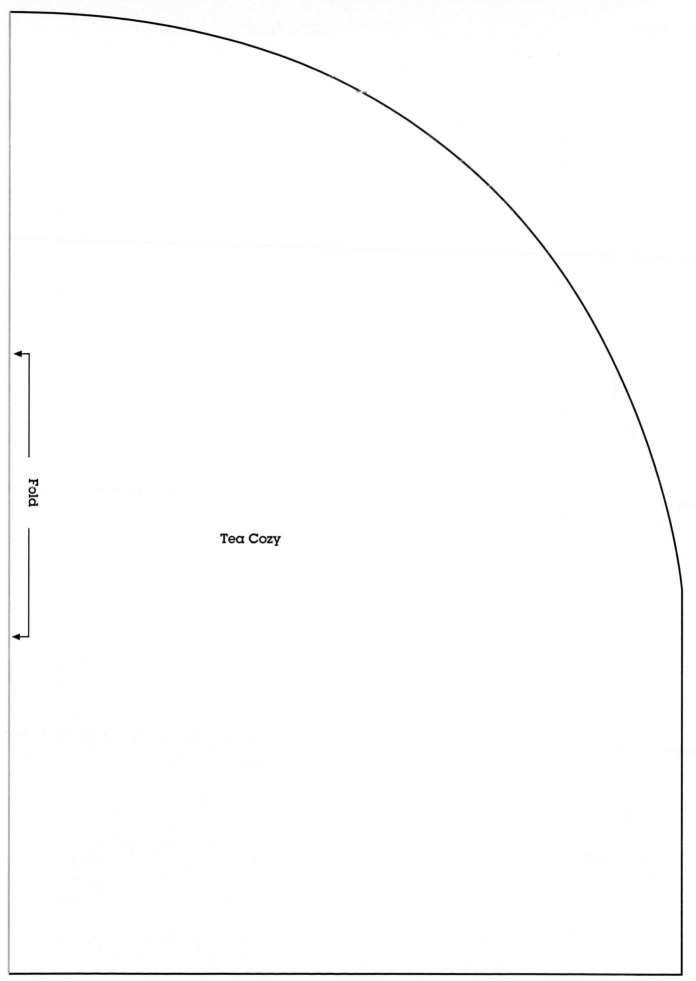

Fold

Tea Cozy

Flower Basket

Petals and patchwork are natural
partners, especially when the
flowers are easy appliqués like
these. Stack them on leaves over
a basket of checked fabric to
complete a country bouquet. Blocks
and casual lettering on the borders
announce a love of baskets and
blooms. This fun wall hanging will
bring garden splendor to any room.

Small Basket Side Borders

Add ¼" seam allowances to ALL templates.

Cutting guide for *each* block – make 10.

Piece	Color	Cut:
A	Basket	1 from template A
No. 1	Tan	1 rectangle 2" x 3½"
No. 2	Basket	1 square 3" x 3"
No. 3	Basket	1 square 2¾" x 2¾"
No. 4	Tan	1 square 2¾" x 2¾"

Appliqué handle (A) to rectangle (No. 1). Cut square (No. 2) once diagonally to make two triangles (you will need one; save the extra for another block). Cut squares (Nos. 3 and 4) twice diagonally to make four triangles from each (you will need 2 of each; save the extras for another block). Referring to the diagram, sew the triangles together to make the bottom half of the basket block; sew it and the appliquéd rectangle (No. 1) together to complete one Small Basket Block.

Repeat to make 10 Small Basket Blocks; sew 5 blocks together to make each side inner border. Sew the borders to the sides of the Basket Block.

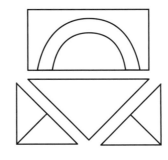

Small Basket Block
Make 10
Finished Size: 3" x 3"

Basket Block

Add ¼" seam allowances to ALL templates.

Cutting guide – make 1.

Piece	Color	Cut;
No. 1	Tan	1 rectangle 12½" x 15½"

Use the templates on pages 8 and 9 for these pieces:

A	Brown	1 from template A
B	Brown	1 from template B
C	Assorted	2 from template C
D	Assorted	2 from template D
E	Red	1 from template E
F	Black	1 from template F
G	Assorted	3 from template G
H	Assorted	3 from template H
I	Green	1 from template I
J	Green	2 from template J
K	Green	4 from template K

Referring to the diagram, appliqué pieces A-K onto the tan background rectangle (No. 1) to make the Basket Block.

Basket Block
Make 1
Finished Size: 12" x 15"

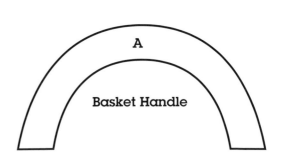

Letter Borders

Add ¼" seam allowances to ALL templates.

Cutting guide for the 12 Letter Blocks.

Piece	Color	Cut:
A	Green	1 from template A
B	Green	1 from template B
E	Green	2 from template E
F	Green	1 from template F
K	Green	1 from template K
L	Green	1 from template L
O	Green	1 from template O
R	Green	1 from template R
S	Green	1 from template S
T	Green	1 from template T
W	Green	1 from template W
No. 1	Tan	12 rectangles 3½" x 4½"
No. 2	Green	2 borders 2½" x 18½"
No. 3	Green	2 borders 2½" x 27½"

Appliqué one letter to each rectangle (No. 1). Referring to the diagram, sew the rectangles together to make the top and bottom inner borders; sew the borders to the center block.

Sew borders (No. 2) to the top and bottom of the center block; sew borders (No. 3) to the sides of the center block to complete the quilt top.

Finishing the Quilt

Layer the quilt top, batting, and backing and quilt as desired. Use 2½" wide bias strips to bind the quilt with double-fold binding. Label the quilt.

Flower Basket Diagram
Finished Size: 22" x 27"

73

Sunshine on the Cabin

Appliquéd stars still shine as golden rays of sunshine appear above this sleepy cabin. The tall pines, shaped by Flying Geese blocks, reach to greet the new day. Below them, fresh-turned garden rows take the shape of our favorite flag. What a peaceful image to start your day!

Sun Block (Section 1)

Follow the instructions on page 48 to make one Sun Block, omitting the appliquéd stars. From grey fabric, cut a 1" x 28¹/₂" strip; sew to bottom edge of Sun Block.

Trees (Sections 2, 3, 4, and 5)

Cutting guide.

Piece	Color	Cut:
No. 1	Creams	31 squares 2⁷/₈" x 2⁷/₈"
No. 2	Greens	31 squares 2⁷/₈" x 2⁷/₈"
No. 3	Dark	1 rectangle 1" x 26¹/₂"
No. 4	Dark	1 rectangle 1" x 22¹/₂"
No. 5	Dark	1 rectangle 1" x 16¹/₂"
No. 6	Dark	1 rectangle 1" x 14¹/₂"
No. 7	Cream	2 rectangles 2¹/₂" x 4¹/₂"
No. 8	Cream	2 rectangles 2¹/₂" x 10¹/₂"
No. 9	Cream	2 squares 2¹/₂" x 2¹/₂"
No. 10	Cream	2 rectangles 1" x 5"
No. 11	Tan	1 square 5" x 5"
No. 12	Tan	1 rectangle 4" x 5"
No. 13	Cream	1 square 5" x 5"
No. 14	Cream	1 rectangle 3" x 5"

Cut each of the squares (Nos. 1 and 2) once diagonally. Sew cream and green triangles together in pairs to make 62 triangle-squares.

Referring to the diagram, sew 22 triangle-squares, rectangles (Nos. 7 and 3), and one rectangle (No. 10) together to make Tree Section 2.

Sew 12 triangle-squares, rectangles (Nos. 4 and 8), and square (No. 11) together to make Tree Section 3.

Sew 14 triangle-squares, rectangles (Nos. 5, 12, and 14), and squares (Nos. 9 and 13) together to make Tree Section 4.

Sew 14 triangle-squares, rectangle (No. 6), and remaining rectangle (No. 10) together to make Tree Section 5.

Stars Block (Section 6)

Cutting guide.

Piece	Color	Cut:
No. 1	Cream	3 squares 4" x 4"
No. 2	Tan	1 rectangle 4" x 11¹/₂"
No. 3	Cream	1 rectangle 4" x 8"
No. 4	Cream	1 rectangle 3¹/₂" x 7¹/₂"
No. 5	Tan	1 square 3¹/₂" x 3¹/₂"
No. 6	Cream	1 rectangle 3¹/₂" x 5"
A	Assorted	4 from template A

Referring to the diagram, sew rectangles and squares (Nos. 1-6) together into vertical rows; sew rows together to make the block. Appliqué 3 stars (A) in place to complete Stars Block. Appliqué remaining star (A) to square (No. 13) in Tree Section 4.

Cabin Block (Section 7)

Add ¹/₄" seam allowances to ALL templates.

Cutting guide – make 1.

Piece	Color	Cut:
No. 1	Cream	3 rectangles 1¹/₂" x 3¹/₂"
No. 2	Black	2 squares 1¹/₂" x 1¹/₂"
No. 3	Cream	1 square 3⁷/₈" x 3⁷/₈
No. 4	Maroon	1 square 3⁷/₈" x 3⁷/₈
No. 5	Maroon	1 square 3¹/₂" x 3¹/₂"
No. 6	Rust	1 rectangle 3¹/₂" x 8¹/₂"
No. 7	Cream	1 square 3¹/₂" x 3¹/₂"
No. 8	Brown	1 rectangle 2¹/₂" x 3¹/₂"
No. 9	Black	1 rectangle 2¹/₂" x 5¹/₂"
No. 10	Brown	2 rectangles 2¹/₂" x 8¹/₂"
No. 11	Brown	3 rectangles 1¹/₂" x 2¹/₂"
No. 12	Black	2 rectangles 1¹/₂" x 2¹/₂"
No. 13	Brown	2 rectangles 3¹/₂" x 5¹/₂"
No. 14	Cream	1 rectangle 1" x 12¹/₂"
No. 15	Tan	1 rectangle 1" x 12¹/₂"
No. 16	Green	1 rectangle 1" x 12¹/₂"
No. 17	Tan	1 rectangle 2¹/₂" x 12¹/₂"

Cut squares (Nos. 3 and 4) once diagonally; sew one triangle of each color together to make a triangle-square (discard remaining triangles). Stitch diagonally, trim, and flip squares (Nos. 4 and 5) to ends of rectangle (No. 6); sew triangle-square and rectangle together.

Referring to the diagram, sew rectangles (No. 1) and squares (No. 2) together. Sew rectangles (Nos. 8 and 9) together and rectangles (Nos. 11 and 12) together. Sew these pieced sections and the remaining rectangles together to complete the Cabin Block.

Flag Block (Section 8)

Cutting guide – make 1.

Piece	Color	Cut:
1	Navy	1 rectangle $3^1/2$" x $9^1/2$"
2	Red	2 stripes $1^1/2$" x $19^1/2$"
3	Red	2 stripes $1^1/2$" x $28^1/2$"
4	Cream	1 stripe $1^1/2$" x $19^1/2$"
5	Cream	2 stripes $1^1/2$" x $28^1/2$"

Referring to the diagram, sew the rectangles together to complete the Flag Block.

Referring to the diagram, sew Sections 1 though 8 of the quilt top together.

Borders

Cutting guide.

Piece	Color	Cut:
No. 1	Black	2 borders $2^1/2$" x $28^1/2$"
No. 2	Black	2 side borders $2^1/2$" x $40^1/2$"
No. 3	Tan	4 squares $2^1/2$" x $2^1/2$"

Sew the top and bottom borders (No. 1) to the quilt top. Sew one square (No. 3) to each end of each border (No. 2); sew to quilt top.

Finishing the Quilt

Layer the quilt top, batting, and backing and quilt as desired. Use $2^1/2$" wide bias strips to bind the quilt with double-fold binding. Label the quilt.

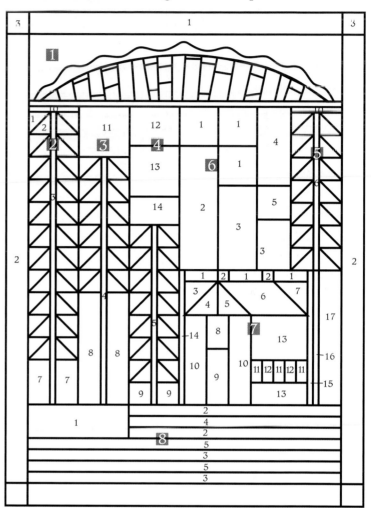

Sunshine On The Cabin Diagram
Finished Size: 32" x 44"

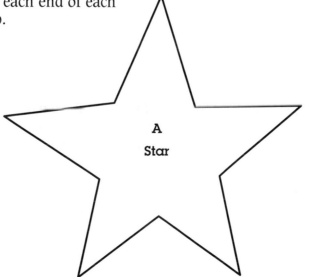

A
Star

79

Through the Garden Window

Such a nice view! Country topiaries gain a touch of whimsy when quilted in playful swirls against a golden sky. This garden window is sure to provide a sunny outlook wherever you hang it.

Borders

From dark green fabric, cut a 6¹/₂" x 21¹/₂" top border, 2 2¹/₂" x 22¹/₂" side borders, and a 2¹/₂" x 17¹/₂" bottom border. Appliqué the arch shape to the top border.

Sew the bottom, side, then top borders to the center section to complete the quilt top.

Finishing the Quilt

Layer the quilt top, batting, and backing and quilt as desired. Use 2¹/₂" wide bias strips to bind the quilt with double-fold binding. Label the quilt.

Topiary Blocks

Referring to the photograph for fabric colors, follow the instructions on page 40 to make 2 Short Topiary Blocks and 1 Tall Topiary Block.

From 1 gold fabric, cut 2 5¹/₂" x 6¹/₂" rectangles for spacers and 1 arch shape from template A (add ¹/₄" seam allowance to A only). Referring to the diagram, sew 1 spacer to the top of each of the Short Topiary Blocks. Sew the 3 topiary blocks together.

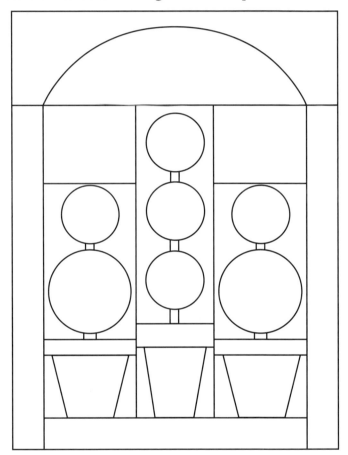

Through the Garden Window Diagram
Finished Size: 21" x 28"

82

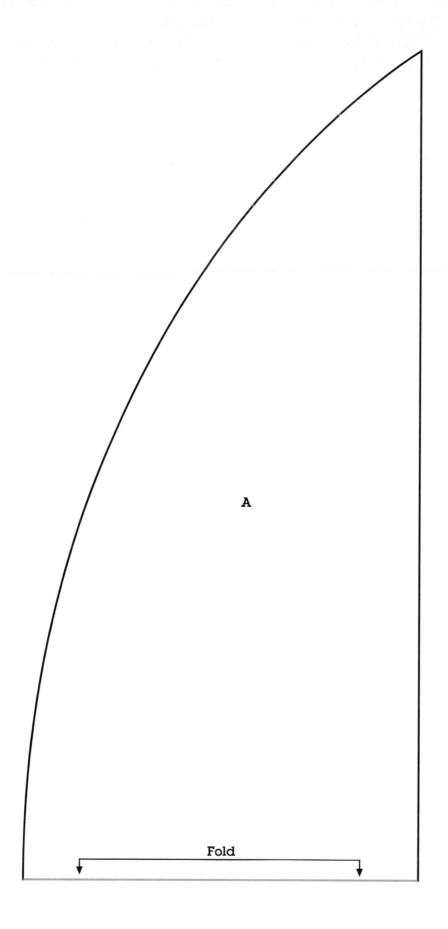

A

Fold

Garden Chair

Some of the best moments of our creative endeavors are when we take a break from stitching or gardening and sit back to admire our handiwork. It's fun to reflect on how tiny seeds become sweet flowers or how patches of soft fabrics become birdhouses and beehives. Every now and then, remember to put down your trowel or your quilting hoop. You've earned the right to just sit a spell.

Chair Block

Referring to the photo for fabric colors, follow the instructions on page 32 to make 1 Chair Block.

Beehive Blocks

Referring to the photo for fabric colors, follow the instructions on page 33 to make 2 Beehive Blocks.

Star Block (template)

Referring to the photo for fabric colors, follow the instructions on page 33 to make 1 Star Block.

1-Hole Birdhouse Blocks

Referring to the photo for fabric colors, follow the instructions on page 18 to make 2 1-Hole Birdhouse Blocks.

2-Hole Birdhouse Blocks

Referring to the photo for fabric colors, follow the instructions on page 18 to make 4 2-Hole Birdhouse Blocks.

Trowel Block

From blue fabric, cut a $4^1/2$" x $8^1/2$" rectangle. Use patterns on page 56 (adding $1/4$" seam allowances) to cut out the pieces for the trowel. Appliqué the pieces to the rectangle to complete the Trowel Block.

Heart Blocks

Referring to the photo for fabric colors, cut a $3^1/2$" x $4^1/2$" rectangle for the small heart background and a $3^1/2$" x $5^1/4$" rectangle for the large heart background. Use the templates (A and B) to cut one small and one large heart (adding $1/4$" seam allowances); appliqué each heart to its background rectangle to complete the Large and Small Heart Blocks.

Star Blocks (appliqué)

Referring to photo for fabric colors, cut 7 squares $4^1/2$" x $4^1/2$". Use template (C) to cut 7 stars (adding $1/4$" seam allowances). Appliqué a star to each square to complete 7 Star Blocks.

Spacers

For spacer above Beehive Blocks, cut a blue rectangle $1^1/2$" x $7^1/2$"; for spacer above Star Block at bottom right corner of quilt top, cut a cream rectangle 2" x $4^1/2$".

Referring to the diagram, sew the blocks and spacers together to make the center section of the quilt top.

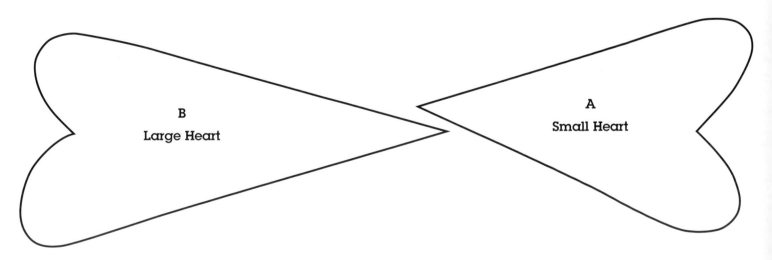

B
Large Heart

A
Small Heart

Borders

From blue fabric, cut 2 1¼" x 19½" strips for the top and bottom inner borders; cut 2 1¼" x 33¾" strips for side inner borders. Sew top and bottom, then side borders to the center section of the quilt top.

From an assortment of blue fabrics, cut several 2½"w strips. From the strips, cut rectangles in varying lengths. Sew the rectangles together to make top and bottom borders 2½" x 21" each. Repeat to make 2 side borders 2½" x 37¾" each. Sew the top and bottom borders, then the side borders to the center section to complete the quilt top.

Finishing the Quilt

Layer the quilt top, batting, and backing and quilt as desired. Use 2½" wide bias strips to bind the quilt with double-fold binding. Label the quilt.

Garden Chair Diagram
Finished Size: 24½" x 37¼"

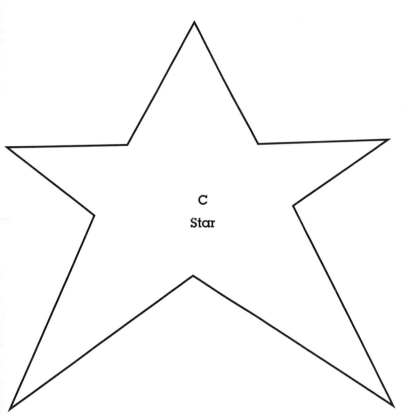

C

Star

87

Bluebirds

It's no wonder that bluebirds are associated with happiness — their friendly, two-note greetings and the flash of their indigo wings are some of the most cheerful things in nature. Why not search your fabric stash for shades of cerulean, sapphire, and azure? With just a bit of stitching, you can bring a little bluebird happiness into your nest!

Bluebirds Blocks and Border

Add ¹/₄" seam allowances to ALL templates.

Piece	Color	Cut:
No. 1	Tan	3 rectangles 4" x 11¹/₂"
No. 2	Cream	1 rectangle 4" x 12¹/₂"
No. 3	Brown	3 strips 1" x 11¹/₂"
No. 4	Brown	1 strip 1" x 12¹/₂"
No. 5	Blue	2 borders 3¹/₂" x 12¹/₂"
No. 6	Blue	2 borders 3¹/₂" x 15¹/₂"
No. 7	Brown	4 squares 3¹/₂" x 3¹/₂"
A	Blue	2 and 2 (R) from template A
B	Black	2 and 2 (R) from template B
C	Gold	2 and 2 (R) from template C
D	Rust	8 from template D
E	Black	4 from template E

To make the pieced rectangles, sew one strip (No. 3) to each rectangle (No. 1) and strip (No. 4) to rectangle (No. 2). Referring to the diagram, appliqué one set of bird pieces (A-C) to each pieced rectangle; sew the rectangles together to make the center section of the quilt top.

Sew one border (No. 5) to each side edge of the quilt top. Sew one square (No. 7) to each end of each border (No. 6); sew borders to top and bottom edges of the quilt top. Appliqué pieces (D and E) onto the borders to complete the quilt top.

Finishing the Quilt

Layer the quilt top, batting, and backing and quilt as desired. Use 2¹/₂" wide bias strips to bind the quilt with double-fold binding. Label the quilt.

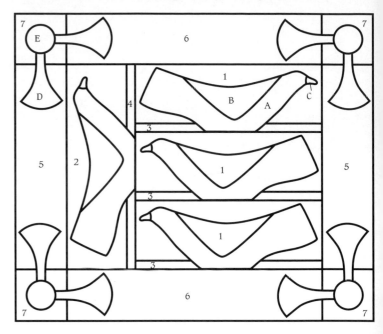

Bluebirds Diagram
Finished Size: 18" x 21"

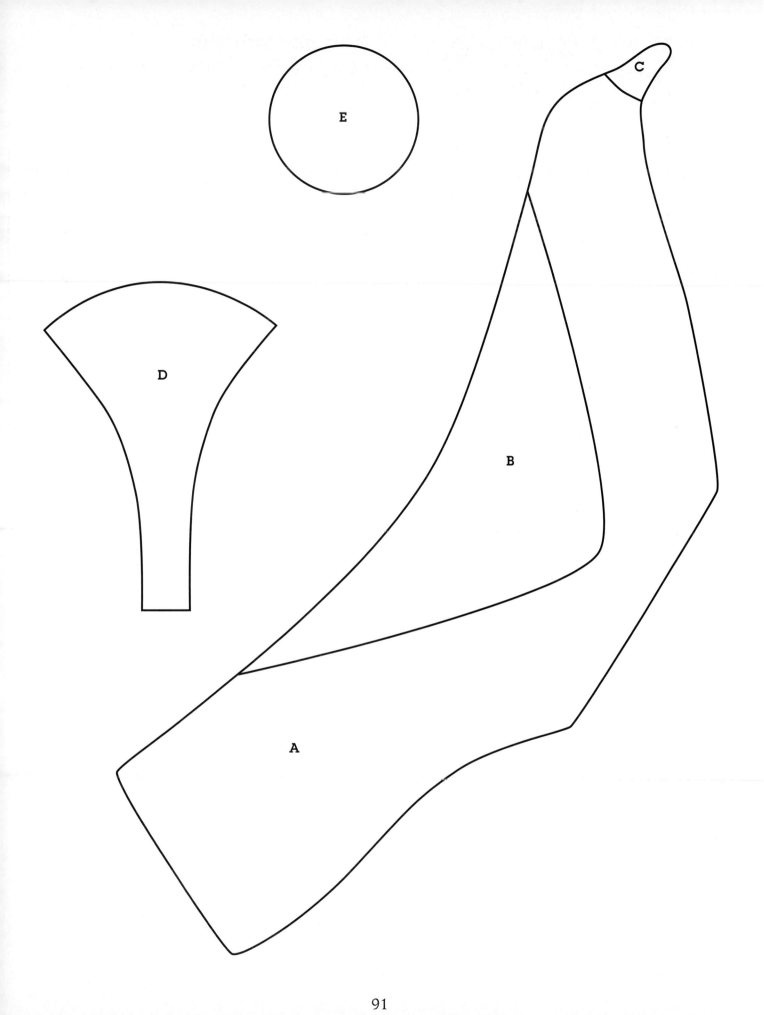

Purple Martin Mansion

These sturdy fruits of the vine are ready to house a gardener's favorite feathered friends. And just as real gourds garner the attention of purple martins, this gentle composition in neutrals catches the human eye with its contrasts of light and dark.

Appliqués

Add ¹/₄" seam allowances to ALL templates.

Cutting guide.

Piece	Color	Cut:
Use the templates on pages 55-57 for these pieces:		
A-C	Tan/Cream	8 from templates A-C
D-F	Black	8 from templates D-F
G-I	Assorted	1 each from templates G-I
J-M	Assorted	1 each from templates J-M

Referring to the diagram, cut the following pieces freehand (sizes are approximate; add seam allowances to measurements given):

N	Rust	1 tree trunk 1¹/₂" x 38"
O	Rust	1 top branch 1" x 20"
P	Rust	1 bottom branch 1" x 23"

Referring to the diagram, appliqué the pieces (A-P) to the background to make the center section of the quilt top.

Borders

Cutting guide.

Piece	Color	Cut:
No. 4	Black	4 strips 1¹/₂" x 44"
No. 5	Brown	4 strips 1¹/₂" x 44"
No. 6	Black	4 squares 2¹/₂" x 2¹/₂"

Sew the black and brown strips (Nos. 4 and 5) together into pairs. From these, cut 68 border segments 2¹/₂" long. Sew 13 segments together for top border; repeat for bottom border. Sew 21 segments and 2 squares (No. 6) together for each side border. Sew the top and bottom, then side borders to the center section to complete quilt top.

Finishing the Quilt

Layer the quilt top, batting, and backing and quilt as desired. Use 2¹/₂" wide bias strips to bind the quilt with double-fold binding. Label the quilt.

Background

Cutting guide.

Piece	Color	Cut:
No. 1	Green	4 rectangles 7¹/₂" x 26¹/₂"
No. 2	Green	1 rectangle 5¹/₂" x 26¹/₂"
No. 3	Green	1 rectangle 9¹/₂" x 26¹/₂"

Referring to the diagram, sew the rectangles (Nos. 1-3) together to make the background.

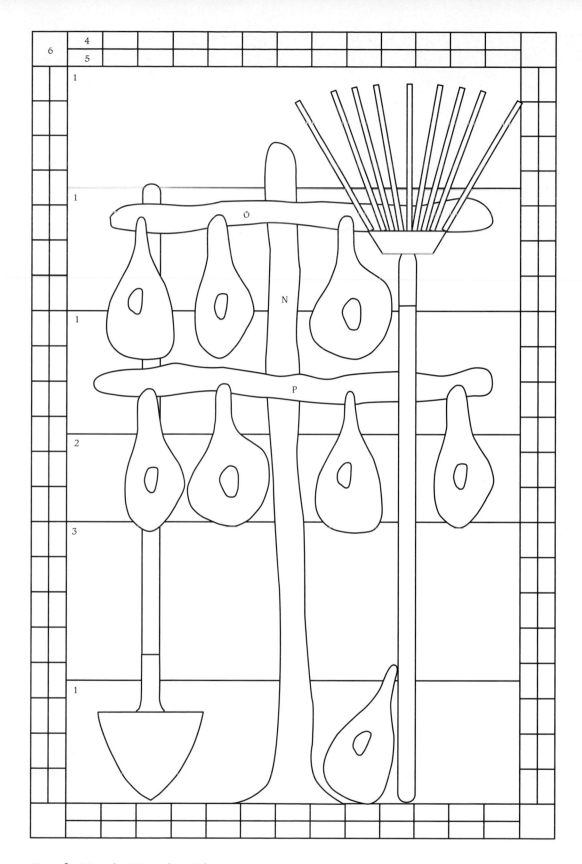

Purple Martin Mansion Diagram
Finished Size: 30" x 46"

Sunflower

Their brown faces haloed
in bright, ray-like petals,
sunflowers are so appropriately
named! Here are a half-dozen of
the fresh-stitched beauties on a
lovely lap quilt. With its warm,
sunny colors, it's perfect
for snuggling under
on a wintry day.

Sunflowers

Referring to photo for fabric selection, follow instructions on page 50 to appliqué a Sunflower to each block background. Sew blocks together to make quilt top.

Borders

Cutting guide – make 1.

Piece	Color	Cut:
No. 4	Creams	2 border strips $1^{1}/_{2}$" x $28^{1}/_{2}$"
No. 5	Creams	36 rectangles $2^{1}/_{2}$" x $4^{1}/_{2}$"
No. 6	Creams	4 squares $2^{1}/_{2}$" x $2^{1}/_{2}$"

Referring to the diagram, sew the border (No. 4) strips to the top and bottom of the quilt top. Sew 11 rectangles (No. 5) together to make each side border. Sew 7 rectangles (No. 5) and 2 squares (No. 6) together to make top border; repeat to make bottom border. Sew side, then top and bottom borders to quilt top.

Finishing the Quilt

Layer the quilt top, batting, and backing and quilt as desired. Use $2^{1}/_{2}$" wide bias strips to bind the quilt with double-fold binding. Label the quilt.

Sunflower Block Backgrounds

Cutting guide for each block – make 6.

Piece	Color	Cut:
No. 1	Creams	4 squares $6^{1}/_{2}$" x $6^{1}/_{2}$"
No. 2	Creams	2 short strips $1^{1}/_{2}$" x $12^{1}/_{2}$"
No. 3	Creams	2 long strips $1^{1}/_{2}$" x $14^{1}/_{2}$"

For each block, sew 4 squares (No. 1) together to make background. Sew short strips (No. 2) to top and bottom of each background; sew long strips (No. 3) to sides of background.

Sunflower Sisters Diagram
Finished Size: 32" x 48"

Garden Path

Everything's springin' up posies on this pretty little quilt. Watering cans are at-the-ready to refresh thirsty flowers. The garden is planted along a trail of blue stepping stones. Because the path makes intriguing turns, "strollers" will look forward to seeing what blooms around the corner. What will you grow along your garden path?

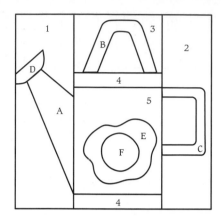

Watering Can Blocks

Add ¹/₄" seam allowances to ALL templates.

Cutting guide for each block – make 2.

Piece	Color	Cut:
No. 1	Cream	1 rectangle 3¹/₂" x 10¹/₂"
No. 2	Cream	1 rectangle 3" x 10¹/₂"
No. 3	Cream	1 rectangle 3¹/₂" x 5"
No. 4	Purple	2 rectangles 1¹/₄" x 5"
No. 5	Purple	1 rectangle 5" x 6"
B	Purple	1 from template B
E	Pink	1 from template E
F	Red	1 from template F

Use patterns on page 15 for the following pieces:

A	Purple	1 from template A
C	Purple	1 from template C
D	Purple	1 from template D

Note - Reverse templates A and D when cutting pieces for second Watering Can Block. Follow instructions on page 14 to make Watering Can Blocks.

Flower Blocks, Spacers and Border

Add ¹/₄" seam allowances to ALL templates.

Cutting guide.

Piece	Color	Cut:
No. 1	Green	6 squares 4¹/₂" x 4¹/₂"
No. 2	Blue	98 rectangles 1¹/₂" x 3¹/₂"
No. 3	Blue	9 rectangles 1¹/₂" x 2¹/₂"
No. 4	Tan	4 squares 3¹/₂" x 3¹/₂"
E	Pinks	6 from template E
F	Pinks	6 from template F
G	Pinks	4 from template G
H	Pinks	4 from template H

Appliqué flower pieces (E and F) to each square (No. 1) to make 6 Flower Blocks. Appliqué flower pieces (G and H) to each square (No. 4) to make 4 Flower Border Squares.

For top border, sew 17 rectangles (No. 2) together; repeat to make bottom border. Sew 22 rectangles (No. 2) together to make each side border. Sew 10 rectangles (No. 2) together to make vertical spacer; repeat to make a total of 2 spacers. Sew 9 rectangles (No. 3) together to make horizontal spacer.

Sew Watering Can Blocks, spacers, and Flower Blocks together to make center section; sew borders and Flower Border Squares to center section to complete quilt top.

Finishing the Quilt

Layer the quilt top, batting, and backing and quilt as desired. Use 2¹/₂" wide bias strips to bind the quilt with double-fold binding. Label the quilt.

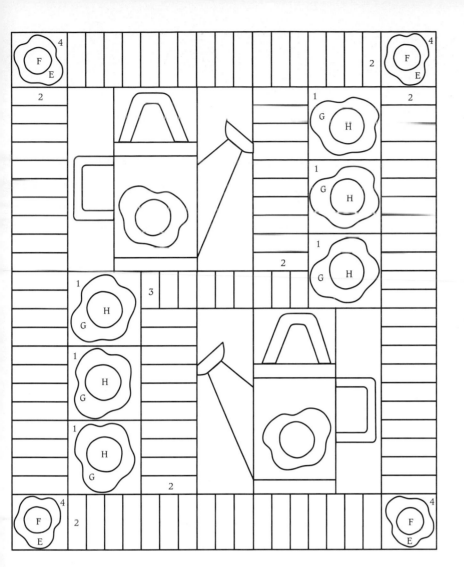

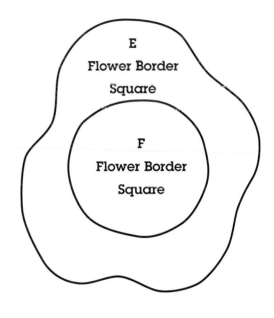

E
Flower Border
Square

F
Flower Border
Square

Garden Path Diagram
Finished Size: 23" x 28"

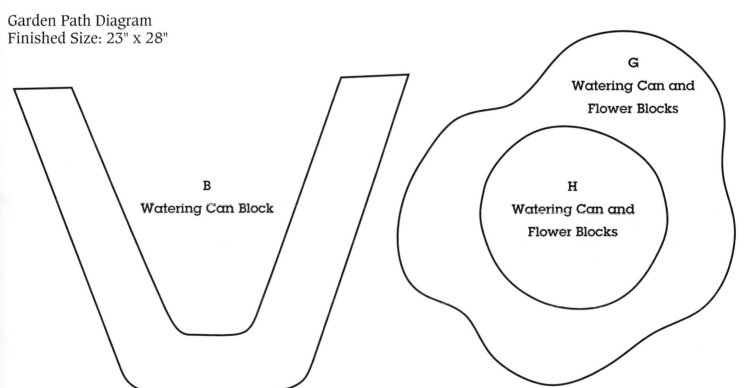

B
Watering Can Block

G
Watering Can and
Flower Blocks

H
Watering Can and
Flower Blocks

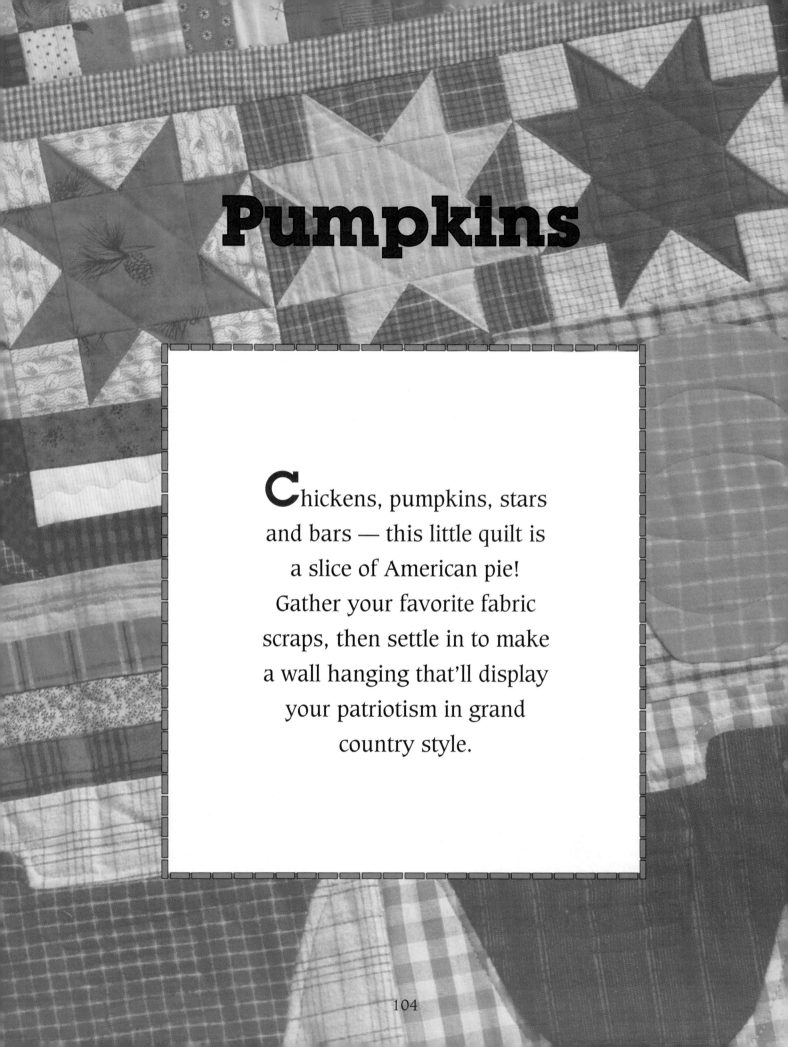

Pumpkins

Chickens, pumpkins, stars and bars — this little quilt is a slice of American pie! Gather your favorite fabric scraps, then settle in to make a wall hanging that'll display your patriotism in grand country style.

Sawtooth Star Blocks

Cutting guide for one block – make 6.

Piece	Color	Cut:
No. 1	Dark	1 square 3" x 3"
No. 2	Dark	8 squares $1^3/4$" x $1^3/4$"*
No. 3	Light	4 rectangles $1^3/4$" x 3"
No. 4	Light	4 squares $1^3/4$" x $1^3/4$"

For each block, use squares (No. 2) and rectangles (No. 3) to make 4 Flying Geese. Assemble the Flying Geese and the remaining squares (Nos. 1 and 4) to make the Sawtooth Star Block.

Flag Block

Add $1/4$" seam allowances to ALL templates.

Cutting guide – make 1.

Piece	Color	Cut:
1-5	Dk. Blue	1 each from templates 1-5
6-9	Lt. Blue	1 each from templates 6-9
No. 10	Red	2 stripes $1^1/2$" x $9^1/2$"
No. 11	Cream	1 stripe $1^1/2$" x $9^1/2$"
No. 12	Red	2 stripes $1^1/2$" x $14^1/2$"
No. 13	Cream	2 stripes $1^1/2$" x $14^1/2$"

Referring to the diagram, sew pieces 1-9 together to make the Star Block; sew the Star Block and the stripes together to make the Flag Block.

Pumpkin Blocks 1 and 2

Add $1/4$" seam allowances to ALL templates.

Cutting guide – make 1.

Piece	Color	Cut:
No. 1	Tan	1 rectangle $6^1/2$" x $7^1/2$"
No. 2	Cream	1 rectangle $5^1/2$" x $7^1/2$"

Use patterns on page 30 for the following pieces:

A	Orange	2 from template A
B	Green	2 from template B

Referring to the diagram, appliqué one piece A and one piece B to each background rectangle (Nos. 1 and 2) to make Pumpkin Blocks 1 and 2.

Chicken Blocks

Add $1/4$" seam allowances to ALL templates.

Cutting guide for each block – make 2.

Piece	Color	Cut:
No. 1	Cream	1 rectangle $8^1/2$" x $10^1/2$"
No. 2	Rust	1 rectangle $1^1/2$" x $10^1/2$"

Use patterns on page 31 for the following pieces:

A	Black	1 from template A
B	Red	1 from template B
C	Gold	1 from template C
D	Green	1 from template D

Note - Reverse templates A through D when cutting pieces for the second Chicken Block. For each block, refer to the diagram to sew the cream (No. 1) and rust (No. 2) rectangles together for background. Appliqué templates A-D onto background.

Heart Block

Add $1/4$" seam allowances to ALL templates.

Cutting guide – make 1.

Piece	Color	Cut:
No. 1	Gold	1 rectangle $3^1/2$" x $5^1/2$"
A	Green	1 from template A

Referring to the diagram, appliqué the heart (A) to the background (No. 1) to make the Heart Block.

Spacers

Cut 2 spacer strips $1^1/2$" x $20^1/2$" from red fabric.

Checkerboard Borders

Cutting guide for 2 borders.

Piece	Color	Cut:
No. 1	Cream	40 squares $1^1/2$" x $1^1/2$"
No. 2	Red	20 squares $1^1/2$" x $1^1/2$"
No. 3	Blue	20 squares $1^1/2$" x $1^1/2$"

Referring to the photo for color placement, sew the squares together into pairs; sew 20 pairs together to make each Checkerboard Border.

Borders

Cutting guide.

Piece	Color	Cut:
No. 1	Black	2 rectangles $2^1/2$" x $20^1/2$"
No. 2	Black	2 rectangles $2^1/2$" x $32^1/2$"
No. 3	Orange	4 squares $2^1/2$" x $2^1/2$"

Referring to the diagram, sew the blocks together; add spacers and borders to complete the Quilt Top.

Finishing the Quilt

Layer the quilt top, batting, and backing and quilt as desired. Use $2^1/2$" wide bias strips to bind the quilt with double-fold binding. Label the quilt.

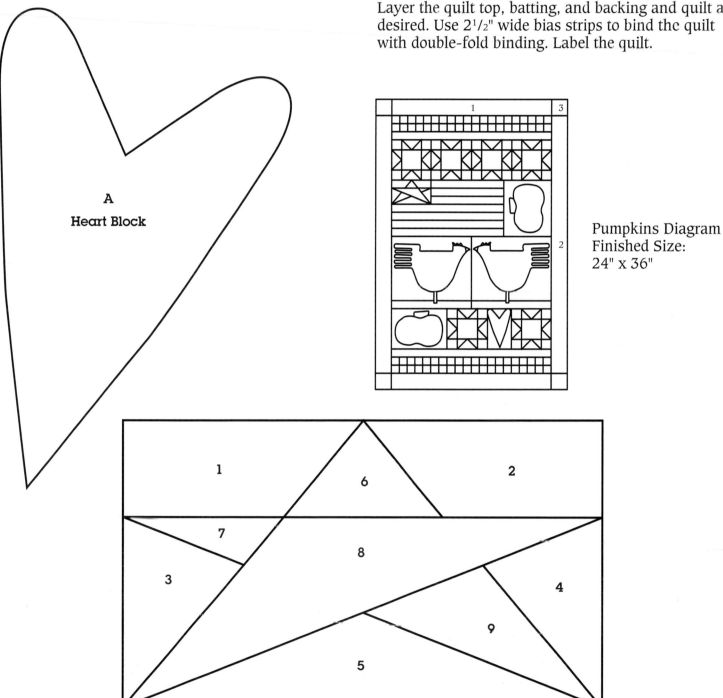

A

Heart Block

Pumpkins Diagram
Finished Size:
24" x 36"

Star Templates 1-9

The Garden Girls of Country Threads

From their broad-brimmed hats to their flowing dresses and comfortable shoes, these ladies are dressed for gardening success. Celebrate your garden-tied friendships with a customized wall hanging of your own — but be prepared! Once your green-thumb associates see themselves captured in fabric, they might each plead for a quilt of their own!

Sashing and Border

Cutting guide.

Piece	Color	Cutting
No. 19	Black	3 rectangles $1^1/_2$" x $12^1/_2$"
No. 20	Black	4 rectangles $1^1/_2$" x $16^1/_2$"
No. 21	Lt. Green	2 squares $1^1/_2$" x $1^1/_2$"
No. 22	Black	2 rectangles $1^1/_2$" x $33^1/_2$"
No. 23	Black	2 rectangles $1^1/_2$" x $40^1/_2$"
No. 24	Black	15 squares $2^7/_8$" x $2^7/_8$"
No. 25	Green	15 squares $2^7/_8$" x $2^7/_8$"
No. 26	Black	2 squares $2^1/_2$" x $2^1/_2$"
No. 27	Black	1 rectangle $2^1/_2$" x $19^1/_2$"
No. 28	Black	1 rectangle $2^1/_2$" x $27^1/_2$"
No. 29	Black	1 rectangle $2^1/_2$" x $32^1/_2$"
No. 30	Black	1 rectangle $2^1/_2$" x $16^1/_2$"

Referring to the diagram, sew Garden Girls Blocks and sashing pieces (Nos. 19-23) together to make the center section of the quilt top. Cut squares (Nos. 24 and 25) once diagonally to make 60 triangles. Sew triangles together in pairs to make 30 triangle-squares. Use the triangle-squares and border pieces (Nos. 26-30) to make borders; sew borders to the center section to complete the Quilt Top.

Garden Girl Blocks

Referring to the photo for fabric selection, follow the instructions on page 44 to make 6 Garden Girl Blocks.

Finishing the Quilt

Layer the quilt top, batting, and backing and quilt as desired. Use $2^1/_2$" wide bias strips to bind the quilt with double-fold binding. Label the quilt.

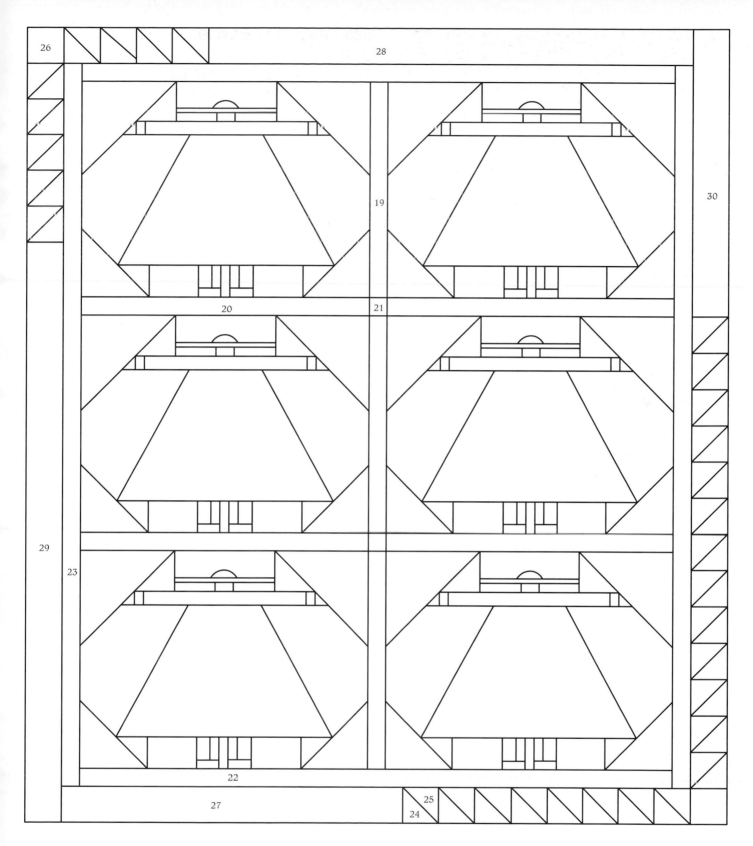

Garden Girls Diagram
Finished Size: 39" x 44"

General Instructions

Complete instructions are given for making each of the quilts and other projects shown in this book. To make your quilting easier and more enjoyable, we encourage you to carefully read all of the general instructions, study the diagrams and color photographs, and familiarize yourself with the individual project instructions before beginning a project.

Quilting Supplies

This list includes all the tools you need for basic quiltmaking, plus additional supplies used for special techniques. Unless otherwise specified, all items may be found in your favorite fabric store or quilt shop.

Batting — Batting is most commonly available in polyester, cotton, or a polyester/cotton blend (see **Choosing and Preparing the Batting**, page 120).

Cutting mat — A cutting mat is a special mat designed to be used with a rotary cutter. A mat that measures approximately 18" x 24" is a good size for most cutting.

Eraser — A soft white fabric eraser or white art eraser may be used to remove pencil marks from fabric. Do not use a colored eraser, as the dye may discolor fabric.

Freezer paper — This heavy, white paper with a wax coating on one side will adhere temporarily to fabric when pressed on with a dry iron.

Iron — An iron with both steam and dry settings and a smooth, clean soleplate is necessary for proper pressing.

Marking tools — There are many different marking tools available (see **Marking Quilting Lines**, page 119). A silver quilter's pencil is a good marker for both light and dark fabrics.

Masking tape — Two widths of masking tape, 1"w and ¼"w, are helpful when quilting. The 1"w tape is used to secure the backing fabric to a flat surface when layering the quilt. The ¼"w tape may be used as a guide when outline quilting.

Needles — Two types of needles are used for hand sewing: *Betweens,* used for quilting, are short and strong for stitching through layered fabric and batting. *Sharps* are longer, thinner needles used for basting and other hand sewing. For *sewing machine needles,* we recommend size 10 to 14 or 70 to 90 universal (sharp-pointed) needles.

Paper-backed fusible web — This iron-on adhesive with paper backing is used to secure fabric cutouts to another fabric when appliquéing. If the cutouts will be stitched in place, purchase the lighter weight web that will not gum up your sewing machine needle. A heavier weight web is used for appliqués that are fused in place with no stitching.

Permanent fine-point pen — A permanent pen is used to mark templates and stencils and to sign and date quilts. Test pen on fabric to make sure it will not bleed or wash out.

Pins — Straight pins made especially for quilting are extra long with large, round heads. Glass head pins will stand up to occasional contact with a hot iron. Some quilters prefer extra-fine dressmaker's silk pins. If you are machine quilting, you will need a large supply of 1" long (size 01) rust-proof safety pins for pin-basting.

Quilting hoop or frame — Quilting hoops and frames are designed to hold the 3 layers of a quilt together securely while you quilt. Many different types and sizes are available, including round and oval wooden hoops, frames made of rigid plastic pipe, and large floor frames made of either material. A 14" or 16" hoop allows you to quilt in your lap and makes your quilting portable.

Rotary cutter — The rotary cutter is the essential tool for quick-method quilting techniques. The cutter consists of a round, sharp blade mounted on a handle with a retractable blade guard for safety. It should be used only with a cutting mat and rotary cutting ruler. Two sizes are generally available; we recommend the larger (45 mm) size.

Rotary cutting ruler — A rotary cutting ruler is a thick, clear acrylic ruler made specifically for use with a rotary cutter. It should have accurate ⅛" crosswise and lengthwise markings and markings for 45° and 60° angles. A 6" x 24" ruler is a good size for most cutting. An additional 6" x 12" ruler or 12½" square ruler is helpful when cutting wider pieces. Many specialty rulers are available that make specific cutting tasks faster and easier.

Scissors — Although much fabric cutting will be done with a rotary cutter, sharp, high-quality scissors are still needed for some cutting. A separate pair of scissors for cutting paper and plastic is recommended. Smaller scissors are handy for clipping threads.

Seam ripper — A good seam ripper with a fine point is useful for removing stitching.

Sewing machine — A sewing machine that produces a good, even straight stitch is all that is necessary for most quilting. Clean and oil your machine often and keep the tension set properly.

Tape measure — A flexible 120" long tape measure is helpful for measuring a quilt top before adding borders.

Template material — Sheets of translucent plastic, often pre-marked with a grid, are made especially for making templates and quilting stencils.

Thimble — A thimble is necessary when hand quilting. Thimbles are available in metal, plastic, or leather and in many sizes and styles. Choose a thimble that fits well and is comfortable.

Thread — Several types of thread are used for quiltmaking: *General-purpose* sewing thread is used for basting, piecing, and some appliquéing. Buy high-quality cotton or cotton-covered polyester thread in light and dark neutrals, such as ecru and grey, for your basic supplies. *Quilting* thread is stronger than general-purpose sewing thread, and some brands have a coating to make them slide more easily through the quilt layers.

Triangle — A large plastic right-angle triangle (available in art and office supply stores) is useful in rotary cutting for making first cuts to "square up" raw edges of fabric and for checking to see that cuts remain at right angles to the fold.

Walking foot — A walking foot or even-feed foot is needed for straight-line machine quilting. This special foot will help all 3 layers of the quilt move at the same rate over the feed dogs to provide a smoother quilted project.

FABRICS
Selecting Fabrics

Choose high-quality, medium-weight, 100% cotton fabrics. All-cotton fabrics hold a crease better, fray less, and are easier to quilt than cotton/polyester blends. All the fabrics for a quilt should be of comparable weight and weave. Check the end of the fabric bolt for fiber content and width.

Preparing Fabrics

All fabrics should be washed, dried, and pressed before cutting.

1. To check colorfastness before washing, cut a small piece of the fabric and place in a glass of hot water with a little detergent. Leave fabric in the water for a few minutes. Remove from water and blot fabric with white paper towels. If any color bleeds onto the towels, wash the fabric separately with warm water and detergent, then rinse until the water runs clear. If fabric continues to bleed, choose another fabric.

2. Unfold yardage and separate fabrics by color. To help reduce raveling, use scissors to snip a small triangle from each corner of your fabric pieces. Machine wash fabrics in warm water with a small amount of mild laundry detergent. Do not use fabric softener. Rinse well and then dry fabrics in the dryer, checking long fabric lengths occasionally to make sure they are not tangling.

3. To make ironing easier, remove fabrics from dryer while they are slightly damp. Refold each fabric lengthwise (as it was on the bolt) with wrong sides together and selvages aligned. If necessary, adjust slightly at selvages so that fold lays flat. Press each fabric with a steam iron set on "Cotton."

ROTARY CUTTING

Based on the idea that you can easily cut strips of fabric and then cut those strips into smaller pieces, rotary cutting has brought speed and accuracy to quiltmaking. Observe safety precautions when using the rotary cutter since it is extremely sharp. Develop a habit of retracting the blade guard *just before* making a cut and closing it *immediately afterward*, before laying down the cutter.

1. Follow **Preparing Fabrics**, page 113, to wash, dry, and press fabrics.

2. Cut all strips from the selvage-to-selvage width of the fabric unless otherwise indicated. Place fabric on the cutting mat, as shown in Fig. 1, with the fold of the fabric toward you. To straighten the uneven fabric edge, make the first "squaring up" cut by placing the right edge of the rotary cutting ruler over the left raw edge of the fabric. Place right-angle triangle (or another rotary cutting ruler) with the lower edge carefully aligned with the fold and the left edge against the ruler (Fig. 1). Hold the ruler firmly with your left hand, placing your little finger off the left edge to anchor the ruler. Remove the triangle, pick up the rotary cutter, and retract the blade guard. Using a smooth, downward motion, make the cut by running the blade of the rotary cutter firmly along the right edge of the ruler (Fig. 2). **Always** cut in a direction **away** from your body and **immediately** close the blade guard after each cut.

Fig. 1

Fig. 2

3. To cut each of the strips required for a project, place the ruler over the cut edge of the fabric, aligning desired marking on the ruler with the cut edge (Fig. 3); make the cut. When cutting several strips from a single piece of fabric, it is important to occasionally use the ruler and triangle to ensure that cuts are still at a perfect right angle to the fold. If not, repeat Step 2 to straighten.

Fig. 3

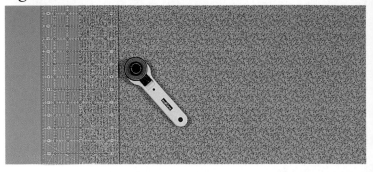

4. To square up selvage ends of a strip before cutting pieces, refer to Fig. 4 and place folded strip on mat with selvage ends to your right. Aligning a horizontal marking on ruler with one long edge of strip, use rotary cutter to trim off selvage to make end of strip square and even (Fig. 4). Turn strip (or entire mat) so that cut end is to your left before making subsequent cuts.

Fig. 4

5. Pieces such as rectangles and squares can now be cut from strips. Usually strips remain folded, and pieces are cut in pairs after ends of strips are squared up. To cut squares or rectangles from a strip, place ruler over left end of strip, aligning desired marking on ruler with cut end of strip. To ensure perfectly square cuts, align a horizontal marking on ruler with one long edge of strip (Fig. 5) before making the cut.

Fig. 5

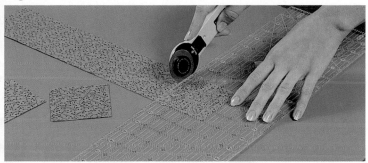

6. To cut two triangles from a square, cut square the size indicated in the project instructions. Cut square once diagonally to make two triangles (Fig. 6).

Fig. 6

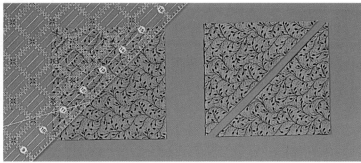

7. To cut four triangles from a square, cut square the size indicated in the project instructions. Cut square twice diagonally to make four triangles (Fig. 7). You may find it helpful to use a small rotary cutting mat so that the mat can be turned to make second cut without disturbing fabric pieces.

Fig. 7

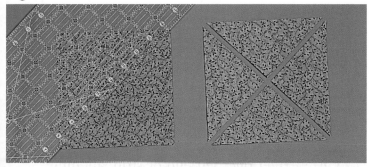

8. After some practice, you may want to try stacking up to 6 fabric layers when making cuts. When stacking strips, match long cut edges and follow Step 4 to square up ends of strip stack. Carefully turn stack (or entire mat) so that squared-up ends are to your left before making subsequent cuts. After cutting, check accuracy of pieces.

9. In some cases, strips will be sewn together into strip sets before being cut into smaller units. When cutting a strip set, align a seam in strip set with a horizontal marking on the ruler to maintain square cuts (Fig. 8). We do not recommend stacking strip sets for rotary cutting.

Fig. 8

10. Most borders for quilts in this book are cut along the more stable lengthwise grain to minimize wavy edges caused by stretching. To remove selvages before cutting lengthwise strips, place fabric on mat with selvages to your left and squared-up end at bottom of mat. Placing ruler over selvage and using squared-up edge instead of fold, follow Step 2 to cut away selvages as you did raw edges (Fig. 9). After making a cut the length of the mat, move the next section of fabric to be cut onto the mat. Repeat until you have removed selvages from required length of fabric.

Fig. 9

11. After removing selvages, place ruler over left edge of fabric, aligning desired marking on ruler with cut edge of fabric. Make cuts as in Step 3. After each cut, move next section of fabric onto mat as in Step 10.

Template Cutting

Our full-sized piecing template patterns do not have a $1/4"$ seam allowance; you must add the seam allowance when making the template. Patterns for appliqué templates also do not include seam allowances. When cutting instructions include (R) after the template designation, place the template upside down on the fabric to cut piece in reverse.

1. To make a template from a pattern, use a permanent fine-point pen to carefully trace pattern onto template plastic, making sure to transfer all alignment and grain line markings. If template is for piecing, use a ruler to add an accurate $1/4"$ seam allowance to each edge of the traced template. Cut out template along outer drawn line. Check template against original pattern for accuracy.

2. To use a piecing template, place template on wrong side of fabric (unless otherwise indicated), aligning grain line on template with straight grain of fabric. Use a sharp fabric-marking pencil to draw around template. Cut out fabric piece using scissors or rotary cutting equipment.

3. To use appliqué templates, place template on right side of the fabric. Use a mechanical pencil with a very fine lead to draw around template on fabric. Use scissors to cut out appliqué a scant $1/4"$ outside drawn line.

PIECING AND PRESSING

Precise cutting, followed by accurate piecing and careful pressing, will ensure that all the pieces of your quilt top fit together well.

Piecing

Set sewing machine stitch length for approximately 11 stitches per inch. Use a new, sharp needle suited for medium-weight woven fabric.

Use a neutral-colored general-purpose sewing thread (not quilting thread) in the needle and in the bobbin. Stitch first on a scrap of fabric to check upper and bobbin thread tensions; make any adjustments necessary.

For good results, it is **essential** that you stitch with an **accurate** $1/4"$ **seam allowance**. On many sewing machines, the measurement from the needle to the outer edge of the presser foot is $1/4"$. If this is the case with your machine, the presser foot is your best guide. If not, measure $1/4"$ from the needle and mark your throat plate with a piece of masking tape. Special presser feet that are exactly $1/4"$ wide are also available for most sewing machines.

When piecing, **always** place pieces **right sides together** and **match raw edges**; pin if necessary. (If using straight pins, remove the pins just before they reach the sewing machine needle.)

Chain Piecing

Chain piecing whenever possible will make your work go faster and will usually result in more accurate piecing. Stack the pieces you will be sewing beside your machine in the order you will need them and in a position that will allow you to easily pick them up. Pick up each pair of pieces, carefully place them together as they will be sewn, and feed them into the machine one after the other. Stop between each pair only long enough to pick up the next and don't cut thread between pairs (Fig. 10). After all pieces are sewn, cut threads, press, and go on to the next step, again chain piecing when possible.

Fig. 10

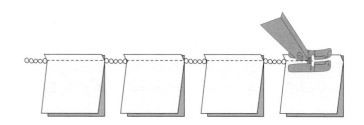

Sewing Set-in Seams

Mark the corner of the piece to be set in with a small dot. To sew the first seam, match right sides and stitch from the outside, stopping and backstitching at the dot (Fig. 11). To sew the second seam, pivot and align remaining edges; stitch again from the outside to the dot and backstitch (Fig. 12).

Fig. 11

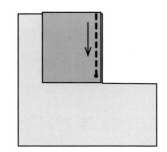

Fig. 12

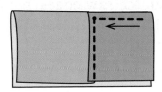

Piecing Template-Cut 5-Point Stars

Follow **Template Cutting**, page 116, and the project instructions to make the templates (adding seam allowances) and cut out the pieces for each 5-Point Star Block.

Referring to Fig. 13, sew pieces 1, 6, and 2 together to make Section A of the Star Block. Sew pieces 3 and 7, then 8 together to make Section B, and pieces 5, 9, and 4 together to make Section C. Sew the sections together to complete the 5-Point Star Block.

Fig. 13

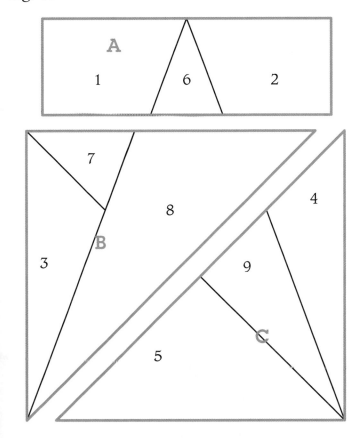

Piecing Flying Geese and Square-in-a-Square Blocks

Use the squares and rectangles specified in the project instructions and refer to Figs. 14 – 18 to make each of the Flying Geese. Place 1 square on one end of one rectangle and stitch diagonally. Trim 1/4" from stitching line and press open.

Place a second square on the opposite end of the rectangle. Stitch diagonally, trim, and press to complete the Flying Geese Block.

To make Square-in-a-Square Blocks, use the same stitch, trim, and flip method to sew a small square to each corner of a larger square.

Fig. 14

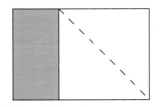

Fig. 15

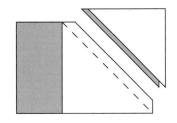

Fig. 16

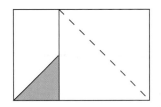

Fig. 17

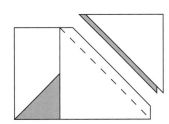

Fig. 18

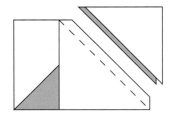

Piecing Sawtooth Star Blocks

Follow Piecing Flying Geese, above, to make 4 Flying Geese Units. Referring to Fig. 19, use the Flying Geese and the additional squares to piece the block by making the 3 horizontal rows then sewing the rows together to complete the Sawtooth Star Block.

Fig. 19

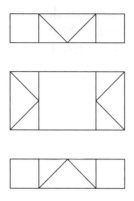

Trimming Seam Allowances

When sewing diamond or triangle pieces together, some seam allowances may extend beyond the edges of the sewn pieces. Trim away these "dog ears" even with the edges of the sewn pieces (Fig. 20).

Fig. 20

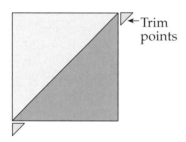

Trim points

Pressing

Use a steam iron set on "Cotton" for all pressing. Press as you sew, taking care to prevent small folds along seamlines. Seam allowances are almost always pressed to one side, usually toward the darker fabric. However, to reduce bulk it may occasionally be necessary to press seam allowances toward the lighter fabric or even to press them open. In order to prevent a dark fabric seam allowance from showing through a light fabric, trim the darker seam allowance slightly narrower than the lighter seam allowance. To press long seams, such as those in long strip sets, without curving or other distortion, lay strips across the width of the ironing board.

NEEDLETURN APPLIQUÉ

In this traditional hand appliqué method, the needle is used to turn the seam allowance under as you sew the appliqué to the background fabric using a **Blind Stitch**, page 125.

1. Place template on right side of appliqué fabric. Use a mechanical pencil with a very fine lead to lightly draw around template, leaving at least 1/2" between appliqués; repeat for number of appliqués specified in project instructions.
2. Cut out shapes a scant 1/4" outside drawn line. Clip inside curves and points up to, but not through, drawn line. Arrange shapes on background fabric and pin or baste in place.
3. Thread a *sharps* needle with a single strand of general purpose sewing thread the color of the appliqué; knot one end.
4. For each appliqué, begin on as straight an edge as possible and use the point of your needle to turn under a short section of seam allowance, concealing drawn line. Use a **Blind Stitch** to stitch the appliqué to the background, turning under the seam allowance and stitching as you continue around the appliqué. Do not turn under or stitch seam allowances that will be covered by other appliqué pieces.
5. Follow **Cutting Away Fabric From Behind Appliqués** to reduce bulk behind appliqués.

Cutting Away Fabric from Behind Appliqués

Hand quilting an appliquéd block will be easier if you are stitching through as few layers as possible. For this reason, or just to reduce bulk in your quilt, you may wish to cut away the background fabric behind appliqués. After stitching appliqués in place, turn block over and use sharp scissors or specially-designed appliqué scissors to trim away background fabric a scant 1/4" from stitching line. Take care not to cut appliqué fabric or stitches.

BORDERS

Borders cut along the lengthwise grain will lay flatter than borders cut along the crosswise grain.

Adding Squared Borders

1. Mark the center of each edge of quilt top.
2. Squared borders are usually added to top and bottom, then side edges of the center section of a quilt top. To add top and bottom borders, measure across center of quilt top to determine length of borders (Fig. 21). Trim top and bottom borders to the determined length.

Fig. 21

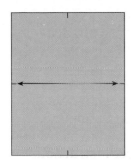

3. Mark center of one long edge of top border. Matching center marks and raw edges, pin border to quilt top, easing in any fullness; stitch. Repeat for bottom border.

4. Measure center of quilt top, including attached borders, to determine length of side borders. Trim side borders to the determined length. Repeat Step 3 to add borders to quilt top (Fig. 22).

Fig. 22

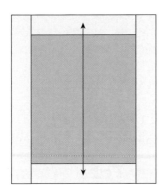

QUILTING

Quilting holds the 3 layers (top, batting, and backing) of the quilt together and can be done by hand or machine. Because marking, layering, and quilting are interrelated and may be done in different orders depending on circumstances, please read the entire **Quilting** section, pages 119 - 122, before beginning the quilting process on your project.

Types of Quilting:

In the Ditch

Quilting very close to a seamline or appliqué is called *"in the ditch"* quilting. This type of quilting does not need to be marked. When quilting in the ditch, quilt on the side of the seam *opposite* the seam allowance.

Outline Quilting

Quilting approximately $1/4$" from a seam or appliqué is called *"outline"* quilting. Outline quilting may be marked, or you may place $1/4$"w masking tape along seamlines and quilt along the opposite edge of the tape. (Do not leave tape on quilt longer than necessary, since it may leave an adhesive residue.)

Ornamental Quilting

Quilting decorative lines or designs is called *"ornamental"* quilting. This type of quilting should be marked before you baste quilt layers together.

Marking Quilting Lines

Fabric marking pencils, various types of chalk markers, and fabric marking pens with inks that disappear with exposure to air or water are readily available and work well for different applications. Lead pencils work well on light-colored fabric, but marks may be difficult to remove. White pencils work well on dark-colored fabric, and silver pencils show up well on many colors. Since chalk rubs off easily, it's a good choice if you are marking as you quilt. Fabric marking pens make more durable and visible markings, but the marks should be carefully removed according to manufacturer's instructions. Press down only as hard as necessary to make a visible line.

When you choose to mark your quilt, whether before or after the layers are basted together, is also a factor in deciding which marking tool to use. If you mark with chalk or a chalk pencil, handling the quilt during basting may rub off the markings. Intricate or ornamental designs may not be practical to mark as you quilt; mark these designs before basting using a more durable marker.

To choose marking tools, take all these factors into consideration and test different markers on scrap fabric until you find the one that gives the desired result.

Using Quilting Stencils

A wide variety of pre-cut quilting stencils, as well as entire books of quilting patterns, are available. Using a stencil makes it easier to mark intricate or repetitive designs on your quilt top.

1. To make a stencil from a pattern, center template plastic over pattern and use a permanent marker to trace pattern onto plastic.
2. Use a craft knife with a single or double blade to cut narrow slits along traced lines (Fig. 23).

Fig. 23

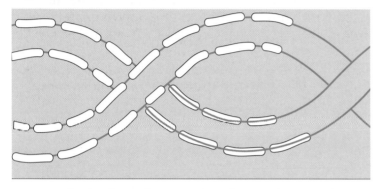

3. Use desired marking tool and stencil to mark quilting lines.

CHOOSING AND PREPARING THE BACKING

To allow for slight shifting of the quilt top during quilting, the backing should be approximately 4" larger on all sides for a bed-size quilt top or approximately 2" larger on all sides for a wall hanging. Yardage requirements listed for quilt backings are calculated for 45"w fabric. If you are making a bed-size quilt, using 90"w or 108"w fabric for the backing may eliminate piecing. To piece a backing using 45"w fabric, use the following instructions.

1. Measure length and width of quilt top; add 8" (4" for a wall hanging) to each measurement.
2. If quilt top is 76"w or less, cut backing fabric into two lengths slightly longer than the determined **length** measurement. Trim selvages. Place lengths with right sides facing and sew long edges together, forming a tube (Fig. 24). Match seams and press along 1 fold (Fig. 25). Cut along pressed fold to form a single piece (Fig. 26).

Fig. 24   Fig. 25

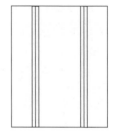

Fig. 26

3. If quilt top is more than 76"w, cut backing fabric into 3 lengths slightly longer than the determined **width** measurement. Trim selvages. Sew long edges together to form a single piece.
4. Trim backing to correct size, if necessary, and press seam allowances open.

CHOOSING AND PREPARING THE BATTING

Choosing the right batting will make your quilting job easier. For fine hand quilting, choose a low-loft batting in any of the fiber types described here. Machine quilters will want to choose a low-loft batting that is all cotton or a cotton/polyester blend because the cotton helps "grip" the layers of the quilt. If the quilt is to be tied, a high-loft batting, sometimes called extra-loft or fat batting, is a good choice.

Batting is available in many different fibers. Bonded polyester batting is one of the most popular batting types. It is treated with a protective coating to stabilize the fibers and to reduce "bearding," a process where batting fibers work their way out through the quilt fabrics. Other batting options include cotton/polyester batting, which combines the best of both polyester and cotton battings; all-cotton batting, which must be quilted more closely than polyester batting; and wool and silk battings, which are generally more expensive and usually only dry-cleanable.

Whichever batting you choose, read the manufacturer's instructions closely for any special notes on care or preparation. When you're ready to use your chosen batting in a project, cut batting the same size as the prepared backing.

LAYERING THE QUILT

1. Examine wrong side of quilt top closely; trim any seam allowances and clip any threads that may show through the front of the quilt. Press quilt top.
2. If quilt top is to be marked before layering, mark quilting lines (see **Marking Quilting Lines**, page 119).
3. Place backing *wrong* side up on a flat surface. Use masking tape to tape edges of backing to surface. Place batting on top of backing fabric. Smooth batting gently, being careful not to stretch or tear. Center quilt top *right* side up on batting.
4. If hand quilting, begin in the center and work toward the outer edges to hand baste all layers together. Use long stitches and place basting lines approximately 4" apart (Fig. 27). Smooth fullness or wrinkles toward outer edges.

Fig. 27

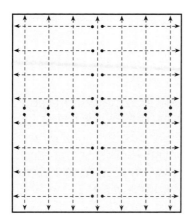

5. If machine quilting, use 1" rust-proof safety pins to "pin-baste" all layers together, spacing pins approximately 4" apart. Begin at the center and work toward the outer edges to secure all layers. If possible, place pins away from areas that will be quilted, although pins may be removed as needed when quilting.

HAND QUILTING

The quilting stitch is a basic running stitch that forms a broken line on the quilt top and backing. Stitches on the quilt top and backing should be straight and equal in length.
1. Secure center of quilt in hoop or frame. Check quilt top and backing to make sure they are smooth. To help prevent puckers, always begin quilting in the center of the quilt and work toward the outside edges.
2. Thread needle with an 18" - 20" length of quilting thread; knot 1 end. Using a thimble, insert needle into quilt top and batting approximately 1/2" from where you wish to begin quilting. Bring needle up at the point where you wish to begin (Fig. 28); when knot catches on quilt top, give thread a quick, short pull to "pop" knot through fabric into batting (Fig. 29).

Fig. 28

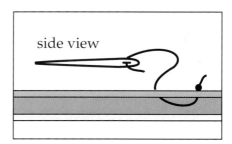

side view

Fig. 29

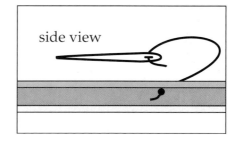

side view

3. Holding the needle with your sewing hand and placing your other hand underneath the quilt, use thimble to push the tip of the needle down through all layers. As soon as needle touches your finger underneath, use that finger to push the tip of the needle only back up through the layers to top of quilt. (The amount of the needle showing above the fabric determines the length of the quilting stitch.) Referring to Fig. 30, rock the needle up and down, taking 3 - 6 stitches before bringing the needle and

thread completely through the layers. Check the back of the quilt to make sure stitches are going through all layers. When quilting through a seam allowance or quilting a curve or corner, you may need to take one stitch at a time.

Fig. 30

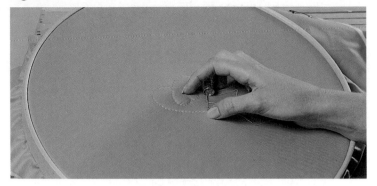

4. When you reach the end of your thread, knot thread close to the fabric and "pop" knot into batting; clip thread close to fabric.

5. Stop and move your hoop as often as necessary. You do not have to tie a knot every time you move your hoop; you may leave the thread dangling and pick it up again when you return to that part of the quilt.

MACHINE STIPPLE QUILTING

The term, "stipple quilting," refers to dense quilting using a meandering line of machine stitching or closely spaced hand stitching. Some projects in this book use machine stipple quilting.

1. Wind your sewing machine bobbin with general-purpose thread that matches the quilt backing. Do not use quilting thread. Thread the needle of your machine with transparent monofilament thread if you want your quilting to blend with your quilt top fabrics. Use decorative thread, such as a metallic or contrasting-colored general-purpose thread, when you want the quilting lines to stand out more.

2. For random stipple quilting, use a darning foot, drop or cover feed dogs, and set stitch length at zero. Pull up bobbin thread and hold both thread ends while you stitch 2 or 3 stitches in place to lock thread. Cut threads near quilt surface. Place hands lightly on quilt on either side of darning foot.

3. Begin stitching in a meandering pattern (Fig. 31), guiding the quilt with your hands. The object is to make stitches of similar length and to not sew over previous stitching lines. The movement of your hands is what determines the stitch length; it takes practice to coordinate your hand motions and the pressure you put on the foot pedal, so go slowly at first.

Fig. 31

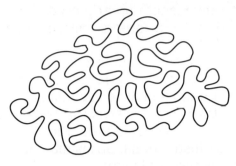

4. Continue machine quilting, filling in one open area of the quilt before moving on to another area, locking thread again at end of each line of stitching by sewing 2 or 3 stitches in place and trimming thread ends.

BINDING

Binding encloses the raw edges of your quilt. Because of its stretchiness, bias binding works well for binding projects with curves or rounded corners and tends to lie smooth and flat in any given circumstance. It is also more durable than other types of binding. Binding may also be cut from the straight lengthwise or crosswise grain of the fabric. You will find that straight-grain binding works well for projects with straight edges.

Making Bias Binding

1. Measure around the edge of the project to be bound and add 12".

2. Cut a sufficient number of $2^{1}/_{2}$"w bias strips to equal the total; trim ends of each strip to a 45° angle. Referring to Fig. 32, sew the strips together to form continuous binding.

Fig. 32

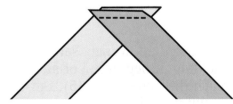

3. Matching wrong sides and raw edges, press bias strip in half lengthwise to complete binding.

Making Straight-Grain Binding

1. To determine length of strip needed if attaching binding with mitered corners, measure edges of the quilt and add 12".
2. To determine lengths of strips needed if attaching binding with overlapped corners, measure each edge of quilt; add 3" to each measurement.
3. Cut lengthwise or crosswise strips of binding fabric the determined length and the width called for in the project instructions. Strips may be pieced to achieve the necessary length.
4. Matching wrong sides and raw edges, press strip(s) in half lengthwise to complete binding.

Attaching Binding with Mitered Corners

1. Press one end of binding diagonally (Fig. 33).

Fig. 33

2. Beginning with pressed end several inches from a corner, lay binding around quilt to make sure that seams in binding will not end up at a corner. Adjust placement if necessary. Matching raw edges of binding to raw edge of quilt top, pin binding to right side of quilt along one edge.
3. When you reach the first corner, mark 1/4" from corner of quilt top (Fig. 34).

Fig. 34

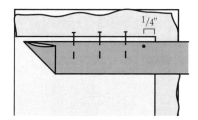

4. Using a 1/4" seam allowance, sew binding to quilt, backstitching at beginning of stitching and when you reach the mark (Fig. 35). Lift needle out of fabric and clip thread.

Fig. 35

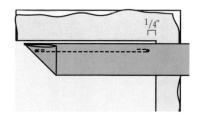

5. Fold binding as shown in Figs. 36 and 37 and pin binding to adjacent side, matching raw edges. When you reach the next corner, mark 1/4" from edge of quilt top.

Fig. 36

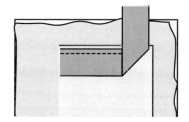

Fig. 37

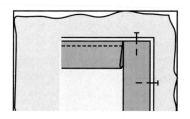

6. Backstitching at edge of quilt top, sew pinned binding to quilt (Fig. 38); backstitch when you reach the next mark. Lift needle out of fabric and clip thread.

Fig. 38

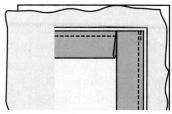

7. Repeat Steps 5 and 6 to continue sewing binding to quilt until binding overlaps beginning end by approximately 2". Trim excess binding.
8. If using 2 1/2"w binding (finished size 1/2"), trim backing and batting a scant 1/4" larger than quilt top so that batting and backing will fill the binding when it is folded over to the quilt backing. If using narrower binding, trim backing and batting even with edges of quilt top.

9. On 1 edge of quilt, fold binding over to quilt backing and pin pressed edge in place, covering stitching line (Fig. 39). On adjacent side, fold binding over, forming a mitered corner (Fig. 40). Repeat to pin remainder of binding in place.

Fig. 39

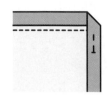

Fig. 40

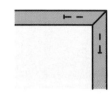

10. Blindstitch binding to backing, taking care not to stitch through to front of quilt.

Attaching Binding with Overlapped Corners

1. Matching raw edges and using a $1/4$" seam allowance, sew a length of binding to top and bottom edges on right side of quilt.
2. If using $2^1/2$"w binding (finished size $1/2$"), trim backing and batting from top and bottom edges a scant $1/4$" larger than quilt top so that batting and backing will fill the binding when it is folded over to the quilt backing. If using narrower binding, trim backing and batting even with edges of quilt top.
3. Trim ends of top and bottom binding even with edges of quilt top. Fold binding over to quilt backing and pin pressed edges in place, covering stitching line (Fig. 41); blindstitch binding to backing.

Fig. 41

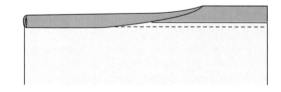

4. Leaving approximately $1^1/2$" of binding at each end, stitch a length of binding to each side edge of quilt. Trim backing and batting as in Step 2.
5. Trim each end of binding $1/2$" longer than bound edge. Fold each end of binding over to quilt backing (Fig. 42); pin in place. Fold binding over to quilt backing and blindstitch in place, taking care not to stitch through to front of quilt.

Fig. 42

MAKING A HANGING SLEEVE

Attaching a hanging sleeve to the back of your wall hanging or quilt before the binding is added allows you to display your completed project on a wall.
1. Measure the width of the wall hanging top and subtract 1". Cut a piece of fabric 7"w by the determined measurement.
2. Press short edges of fabric piece $1/4$" to wrong side; press edges $1/4$" to wrong side again and machine stitch in place.
3. Matching wrong sides, fold piece in half lengthwise to form a tube.
4. Follow project instructions to sew binding to quilt top and to trim backing and batting. Before blindstitching binding to backing, match raw edges and stitch hanging sleeve to center top edge on back of wall hanging.
5. Finish binding wall hanging, treating the hanging sleeve as part of the backing.
6. Blindstitch bottom of hanging sleeve to backing, taking care not to stitch through to front of quilt.
7. Insert dowel or slat into hanging sleeve.

SIGNING AND DATING YOUR QUILT

Your completed quilt is a work of art and should be signed and dated. There are many different ways to do this, and you should pick a method that reflects the style of the quilt, the occasion for which it was made, and your own particular talents.
The following suggestions may give you an idea for recording the history of your quilt for future generations.
• Embroider your name, the date, and any additional information on the quilt top or backing. You may choose floss colors that closely match the fabric you are working on, such as white floss on a white border, or contrasting colors may be used.
• Make a label from muslin and use a permanent marker to write your information. Your label may be as plain or as fancy as you wish. Then stitch the label to the back of the quilt.
• Chart a cross-stitch label design that includes the information you wish and stitch it in colors that complement the quilt. Stitch the finished label to the quilt backing.

EMBROIDERY STITCHES

Straight Stitch

Come up at 1 and go down at 2 (Fig. 43). Length of stitches may be varied as desired.

Fig. 43

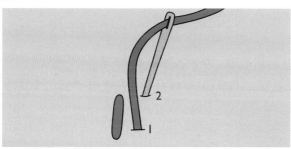

Stem Stitch

Come up at 1. Keeping thread below the stitching line, go down at 2 and come up at 3. Go down at 4 and come up at 5 (Fig. 44).

Fig. 44

Satin Stitch

Come up at 1; go down at 2 and come up at 3. Continue until area is filled (Fig. 45).

Fig. 45

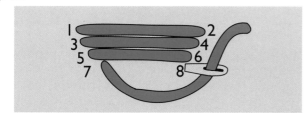

Running Stitch

The running stitch consists of a series of straight stitches with the stitch length equal to the space between stitches (Fig. 46).

Fig. 46

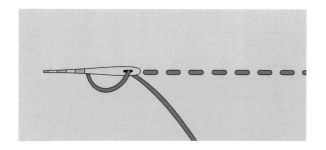

Blanket Stitch

Come up at 1. Go down at 2 and come up at 3, keeping thread below point of needle (Fig. 47). Continue working as shown in Fig. 48.

Fig. 47

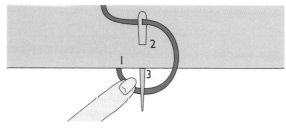

Fig. 48

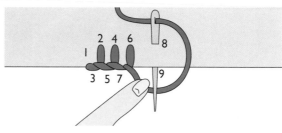

Blind Stitch

Come up at 1. Go down at 2 and come up at 3 (Fig. 49). Length of stitches may be varied as desired.

Fig. 49

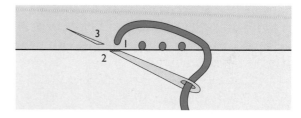

French Knot

Come up at 1. Wrap thread once around needle and insert needle at 2, holding end of thread with non-stitching fingers (Fig. 50). Tighten knot; then pull needle through, holding floss until it must be released. For larger knot, use more strands; wrap only once.

Fig. 50

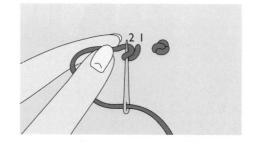

GLOSSARY

Appliqué — A cutout fabric shape that is secured to a larger background. Also refers to the technique of securing the cutout pieces.

Backing — The back or bottom layer of a quilt, sometimes called the "lining."

Backstitch — A reinforcing stitch taken at the beginning and end of a seam to secure stitches.

Basting — Large running stitches used to temporarily secure pieces or layers of fabric together. Basting is removed after permanent stitching.

Batting — The middle layer of a quilt that provides the insulation and warmth as well as the thickness.

Bias — The diagonal (45° for true bias) grain of fabric in relation to crosswise or lengthwise grain (see Fig. 51).

Binding — The fabric strip used to enclose the raw edges of the layered and quilted quilt. Also refers to the technique of finishing quilt edges in this way.

Blindstitch — A method of hand sewing an opening closed so that it is invisible.

Border — Strips of fabric that are used to frame a quilt top.

Chain piecing — A machine-piecing method consisting of joining pairs of pieces one after the other by feeding them through the sewing machine without cutting the thread between the pairs.

Grain — The direction of the threads in woven fabric. "Crosswise grain" refers to the threads running from selvage to selvage. "Lengthwise grain" refers to the threads running parallel to the selvages (Fig. 51).

Fig. 51

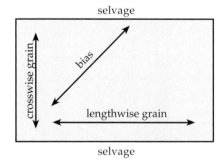

Machine baste — To baste using a sewing machine set at a long stitch length.

Miter — A method used to finish corners of quilt borders or bindings consisting of joining fabric pieces at a 45° angle.

Piecing — Sewing together the pieces of a quilt design to form a quilt block or an entire quilt top.

Pin basting — Using rust-proof safety pins to secure the layers of a quilt together prior to machine quilting.

Quilt block — Pieced or appliquéd sections that are sewn together to form a quilt top.

Quilt top — The decorative part of a quilt that is layered on top of the batting and backing.

Quilting — The stitching that holds together the 3 quilt layers (top, batting, and backing); or, the entire process of making a quilt.

Sashing — Strips or blocks of fabric that separate individual blocks in a quilt top.

Seam allowance — The distance between the seam and the cut edge of the fabric. In quilting, the seam allowance is usually ¹/₄".

Selvages — The 2 finished lengthwise edges of fabric (see Fig. 51). Selvages should be trimmed from fabric before cutting.

Set (or Setting) — The arrangement of the quilt blocks as they are sewn together to form the quilt top.

Setting squares — Squares of plain (unpieced) fabric set between pieced or appliquéd quilt blocks in a quilt top.

Setting triangles — Triangles of fabric used around the outside of a diagonally-set quilt top to fill in between outer squares and border or binding.

Stencil — A pattern used for marking quilting lines.

Straight grain — The crosswise or lengthwise grain of fabric (see Fig. 51). The lengthwise grain has the least amount of stretch.

Strip set — Two or more strips of fabric that are sewn together along the long edges and then cut apart across the width of the sewn strips to create smaller units.

Template — A pattern used for marking quilt pieces to be cut out.

Triangle-square — In piecing, 2 right triangles joined along their long sides to form a square with a diagonal seam (Fig. 52).

Fig. 52

Unit — A pieced section that is made as individual steps in the quilt construction process are completed. Units are usually combined to make blocks or other sections of the quilt top.